Usability Evaluation
of Modeling Languages

Christian Schalles

Usability Evaluation of Modeling Languages

An Empirical Research Study

Foreword by Prof. Dr. Michael Rebstock
and Dr. John Creagh

 Springer Gabler

RESEARCH

Christian Schalles
Leidersbach, Germany

Dissertation Cork Institute of Technology (Ireland), 2012

ISBN 978-3-658-00050-9   ISBN 978-3-658-00051-6 (eBook)
DOI 10.1007/978-3-658-00051-6

Library of Congress Control Number: 2012947015

The Deutsche Nationalbibliothek lists this publication in the Deutsche Nationalbibliografie; detailed bibliographic data are available in the Internet at http://dnb.d-nb.de.

Springer Gabler
© Springer Fachmedien Wiesbaden 2013

Printed on acid-free paper

Springer Gabler is a brand of Springer DE. Springer DE is part of Springer Science+Business Media.
www.springer-gabler.de

To Carina, Heidi, Wilhelm and Andreas. Thanks for your
patience and support

Foreword

Conceptual modeling often is considered to be at the heart of the Business and Information Systems Engineering discipline. Without conceptual modeling, it would be extraordinarily costly and time-consuming, if not impossible, to communicate concepts, structures and artifacts of a project domain between a larger number of team members and to finish a project successfully and efficiently. Graphical modeling languages are the key instruments of conceptual modeling and are widely used not only throughout most diverse kinds of software projects, but also in process management, quality management or compliance management projects.

Compared to its central importance, surprisingly little is known about the usability evaluation of modeling languages. Graphical modeling languages are invented and developed by persons, teams or organizations, often based upon prior concepts, and can evolve into being a certified or a *de facto* industry standard. But during these development processes, usability evaluations are not yet common. Thus it often remains unclear, when a language should be chosen for a given project task, what intellectual and practical skills the use of the concepts and elements of the language requires, or which aspects influence the content and the quality of models developed. Still, these questions are of considerable relevance for the success of modeling tasks in organizational practice.

Christian Schalles investigates and sheds light on this exciting and important, however rather neglected field of research. For this purpose he examines the variables that influence the usability of modeling languages. His inquiry not only brings together conceptual arguments, but is also driven by empirical research. In an innovative way, the usability evaluation concept presented in this book combines approaches from different disciplines. Relevant usability attributes are derived from literature; metrics and a framework for evaluation are developed; hypotheses are formulated and tested empirically. Thus, usability evaluation of graphical modeling languages is put on a sound basis.

The book not only widens and enhances research about modeling languages and sets an agenda for future investigation. It is also of immediate use for developers of graphical modeling languages, as it contains recommendations for the refinement of existing languages or the development of new ones – wherever this, despite the plethora on hand, may still be necessary. It is also useful for business practice, as it provides a decision framework that helps project managers to determine the appropriate modeling language for a given application context. I hope that the book will be well received by the different audiences it addresses and that it spurs many fruitful discussions in research teams, standardization bodies, public administrations and businesses.

Prof. Dr. Michael Rebstock

June, 2012

Foreword

This thesis explores the usability of modeling languages used in both software development and business processes. A Framework for Usability Evaluation of Modeling Languages (FUEML) is developed, followed by a series of investigations based on FUEML.

This research into the usability of modeling languages has significant implications for the future evolution of modeling languages both in software development and business processes. With a greater understanding of user experiences, software tools may present an environment for model development and interpretation that leads to greater efficiency and effectiveness.

The overall approaches taken by this research in the development of a framework may be a beneficial approach for many other areas where usability is important.

The Department of Computing at the Cork Institute of Technology, Ireland (CIT) has a long established collaboration with the University of Applied Sciences in Darmstadt.

This Ph.D. thesis was successfully completed by Christian Schalles, under the supervision of Dr. John Creagh, Department of Computing, CIT, and Prof. Dr. Michael Rebstock, Faculty of Business Administration and Economics, Darmstadt

I wish to express my gratitude to the Cork Institute of Technology and the University of Applied Sciences Darmstadt.

Dr. John Creagh

Cork Institute of Technology June, 2012

Acknowledgements

It would not have been possible to write this doctoral thesis without the help and support of the kind people around me, to only some of whom it is possible to give particular mention here.

In the first place, I wish to thank the members of the supervision team for their positive and comprehensive support and encouragement over the last years.

Dr. John Creagh, who supported this work as the main supervisor. He supervised me at the Cork Institute of Technology. Thank you very much for your supervision during the last years.

Prof. Dr. Michael Rebstock, who supervised me at the University of Applied Sciences Darmstadt. Thank you very much for your supervision.

Furthermore, I wish to thank the Cork Institute of Technology and especially Michael Loftus and Jim O'Dwyer.

I also would like to acknowledge the contribution of Holger Bassarek, who assisted with his vast knowledge in eye-tracking hardware and software.

Thanks must also be given to my research group at the University of Applied Sciences Darmstadt: Kerstin Reinking, Emanuel Berger, Janina Fengel and Walter Noll. Thank you for your support in all that years.

I would specially like to thank Prof. Dr. Udo Bleimann from the University of Applied Sciences Darmstadt and Dr. Ingo Stengel from the University of Plymouth who supported me in formal and informal issues around my PhD.

This is also extended to Normen Haas and Tilman Swinke from the University of Applied Sciences Worms. Thanks guys for a great time in Cork in January 2011. Good luck with your PhD!

I also want to thank Prof. Dr. Christoph Wiese for his mental support during the time of my PhD-studies.

Last, but by no means least, I thank my friends in Ireland, Great Britain, Germany and elsewhere for their support and encouragement throughout, some of whom have already been named.

Keep on rockin' guys!

Dr. Christian Schalles

June, 2012

Abstract

Over the last two decades more and more companies started to recognize the importance of graphical modeling as a way to meet their business goals. In order to describe a business case such as a business process or an application system, information in various different formats has to be integrated within a graphical model. Graphical models are developed using modeling languages such as the Unified Modeling Language (UML) and Event Driven Process Chains (EPC).

The usability of graphical modeling languages has not been explicitly considered in past research. Most usability evaluation surveys are mainly focusing on applications, websites, software and technical products. Usability has not been focused on within the development of current graphical languages for conceptual modeling. Consequently, the impact of graphical modeling languages on users as well as the output resulting from their application is not clear.

This thesis focuses on an empirical usability evaluation of graphical modeling languages in business process and software modeling. A usability evaluation framework for graphical modeling languages is proposed. The framework contains different user scenarios, usability attributes and metrics for measuring usability in the domain of graphical modeling languages.

Based on this, hypotheses assuming differences of various graphical modeling languages regarding their impact on usability are developed. Subsequently, the defined hypotheses are explored by the conduction of an empirical survey. The data analysis is calculated by using an Analysis of Covariance (ANCOVA) and a Structural Equation Modeling (SEM) approach for analyzing causal interactions and relations between language and usability attributes.

General empirical findings of this thesis are that language-based metaproperties such as complexity and visual properties of graphical modeling languages influence the usability on different causal stages. Furthermore, it is empirically proven that two differing scenarios, the model development scenario and the model interpretation scenario affect usability in separate ways.

Subsequently, the empirical results are applied for developing a management decision framework supporting CIOs in industry with the user-oriented selection of modeling languages suitable to company's requirements. In addition to that, the process of modeling in companies is determined and enriched with the findings of the empirical surveys conducted in this thesis.

This thesis provides important findings for modeling language standardization and development organizations as well as practitioners from industry.

Contents

III. RESUME OF THE EMPIRICAL RESULTS   137

9. Further Processing of the Empirical Results   139

10. Principles for Future Development of graphical Modeling Languages   147

IV. CONCLUSION AND OUTLOOK 151

List of Figures

List of Tables

Part I.

INTRODUCTION AND BACKGROUND

1. Introduction

Application and business process modeling has received considerable attention recently by both business administration and computer science communities. Modeling has always been at the core of organizational design and information systems development. Models enable decision-makers to filter out the irrelevant complexities of the real world so that efforts can be directed towards the most important parts of the system or business process under study.

However, both business analysts and information system professionals may find it difficult to navigate through a maze of theoretical paradigms, methodological approaches, and representational formalisms that have been proposed for business process modeling and information systems modeling.

The aim of the study presented in this thesis is to analyze the usability of existing visual modeling formalisms, i.e. graphical modeling languages.

1.1. Motivation

Complex software systems form the basis of the modern information society. Software engineering is about developing, maintaining and managing high-quality software systems in a cost-effective and predictable way [Sjoberg et al., 2007].

Modeling is a concept fundamental for software engineering and business process management. Models can be found in all areas and applications of software engineering [Ludewig, 2003].

For accurate interpretation it is important that a model reproduces the knowledge contained in a clearly arranged and well-structured manner. To ensure this, users need to understand the model, i.e., they have to be familiar with the modeling language used [Mendling and Strembeck, 2008].

In organizations, models are important for documenting business processes and specifying information system requirements under development. Models are represented by using graphical modeling languages such as the Business Process Modeling Notation (BPMN), Event Driven Process Chains (EPC) and the Unified Modeling Language (UML) providing a set of elements, relations and rules for combining them.

The research presented in this thesis focuses on the usability evaluation of graphical modeling languages established in software engineering and business process modeling.

Avison and Fitzgerald (1995) defined the two main reasons for evaluating graphical modeling languages [Avison and Fitzgerald, 1995]:

1. The academic reason is to better understand the nature of modeling languages in order to improve future modeling languages development.

2. The practical reason is to support the customizing process and the decision process for or against specific modeling languages in companies.

In general, graphical modeling languages aim to support the expression of relevant aspects of real world domains such as business processes or application system structures [Sjoberg et al., 2007].

Previous research has focused on the evaluation of technical and functional aspects of graphical modeling languages. Just a few number of researchers connect their evaluation studies with the user of modeling languages [Birkmeier et al., 2010].

In this thesis the connection between modeling languages and users is investigated. Furthermore, a theoretical framework defining usability in the domain of graphical modeling languages is developed. Based on this two empirical surveys prove the quality of the developed evaluation framework and explore important findings about the impact of modeling languages on usability.

1.2. Research Question

Concerning a usability evaluation of graphical modeling languages it is necessary to define clear structured research questions underlining the aim of the presented research.

First, a short subsumption of current user-oriented surveys in the modeling domain is offered. Based on this, the research questions are defined.

Recker and Dreiling (2007) conducted a survey on understanding process modeling languages including EPC's and BPMN. They deal with the investigation of how learning affects modeling works. Particularly, this empirical study focuses on the interpretation of diagrams developed with EPC's and BPMN and comes up with the result that process modellers with training in any process modeling language perform reasonably well in understanding other unknown process models [Recker and Dreiling, 2007].

Mendling and Strembeck (2008) analyzed influence factors of understanding business process models with applying an online questionnaire [Mendling and Strembeck, 2008]. The results of this survey support the hypothesis that personal, model and content related factors influence the understandability of process models.

Siau and Rossi (2007) identified a lack of empirical evaluation considering practical scenarios. Furthermore they strongly propose further surveys to study the usability of modeling languages [Siau and Rossi, 2008].

Mendling and Strembeck (2008) recommend future surveys for analyzing the understandability of process models [Mendling and Strembeck, 2008].

Overhage and Schlauderer (2010) compared the usability of BPMN and UML Activity diagrams based on the Bunge-Weber-Wand Ontology [Birkmeier et al., 2010].

Daniel L. Moody and his research group analyzed the physics and visual syntax of graphical modeling languages theoretically [Moody, 2004, Moody and Hillegersberg, 2009, Moody, 2009, Moody and Heymans, 2010]. They did not support their findings with the conduction of empirical surveys.

As the analyzed related work has shown, previous studies are mainly evaluating partitions of usability regarding modeling languages. The presented related past research activities show a current research need for an overall survey evaluating the usability of graphical modeling languages.

The first research question focuses on the thesis that different modeling concepts influence usability in different ways. Both behavioural and structural modeling need to be investigated. Past and current research has not focused on this question intensely. The answer to this main research question is given in chapter 6 of this thesis.

The second research question has a causal character and aims to specify the way different modeling languages impact different usability attributes. The answer for this question is given in chapter 8 of this thesis.

It is possible to deduce **further questions** based on the presented two main research questions:

- How can usability be measured in the domain of graphical modeling languages?

    - What are properties of modeling languages, which influence the usability attributes? How can they be measured?

    - Do different user scenarios exist, which influence the usability of graphical modeling languages?

    - Do further language-independent variables exist that influence the usability of graphical modeling languages?

These questions are answered within the development of a usability evaluation framework in the domain of graphical modeling languages. The framework is presented in chapter 4 of this thesis. The following figure shows the defined main research questions and their connected deductions.

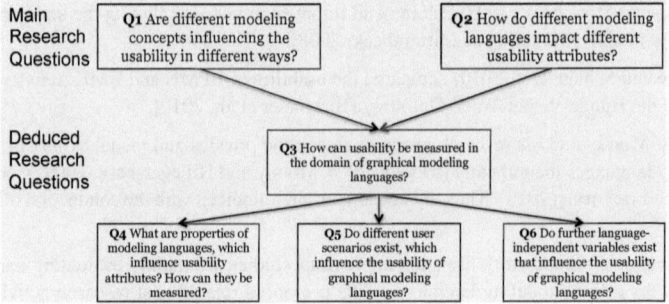

Figure 1.2.1.: Research Questions and Deductions

1.3. Structure

The general structure of this thesis is similar to an empirical research thesis.

Chapter 2 defines the theoretical background for graphical modeling and connected modeling languages.

In chapter 3 necessary theories acting as a background for the empirical surveys are defined. Due to the fact, that those theories are mainly user and usability-oriented, the underlain theories have their traditional roots in psychology.

Chapter 4 presents the development of a framework for usability evaluation of graphical modeling languages. This chapter acts as a basis chapter of this thesis. All forthcoming empirical studies are based on this evaluation framework.

Chapter 5 deals with the development of a generic metric for measuring model complexity. In the further course of this thesis it becomes clear, that model complexity acts as a significant interfering variable. Consequently, a method for measuring model complexity has to be developed. Thus, the influence of model complexity in the upcoming empirical surveys is considered.

In chapter 6 the presented evaluation framework is applied. Therefore, hypotheses, survey design, data collection, data analysis and implications are presented.

Chapter 7 focuses on challenges when using a specific statistical approach for analyzing causal relations between several statistical constructs within the scope of the presented research.

The application and realization of a structural equation modeling approach is presented in chapter 8. Concerning this, hypotheses, structural models, measurement models, data analysis and data interpretation are included in this chapter.

In chapter 9 the results of the empirical surveys are represented and summarized. Furthermore, a management decision framework supporting the selection process for or against specific

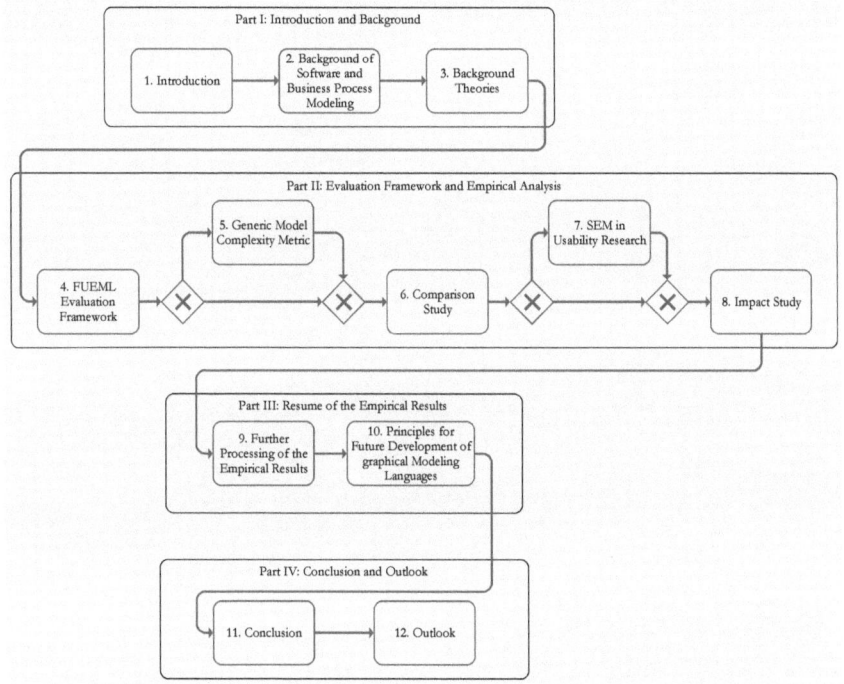

Figure 1.3.1.: Structure of this Book - Recommended Reading Process

modeling languages in enterprises is developed and presented. This framework is based on specific experiences and outcomes of the conducted research presented in this thesis.

Chapter 10 gives structured recommendations for the future development of graphical modeling languages.

The last chapter deals with a short summary and proposes further research based on the results and findings of this thesis.

2. Background of Software and Business Process Modeling

This chapter introduces the term of modeling especially in the domains of software engineering and business process management. Therefore, the general concept of modeling and the history of modeling in enterprises is subsumed and introduced. Furthermore, important and for this thesis relevant terms in the modeling domain are defined and pictured regarding their semantic correspondence. The survey in this thesis aims to be a cross-language survey over different modeling concepts. Therefore, the similarities of different modeling concepts and consequently the similarity of resulting languages are defined. In a nutshell, the following chapter shows the general view and understanding of modeling applied in this thesis.

2.1. General Concept of Modeling

The term "model" is derived from the Latin word modulus, which means measure, rule or pattern. Obvious examples are toy railways and dolls, maps as well as architectural models of buildings.

In the domain of enterprise modeling, process models, design patterns and architectural diagrams exist. Other models are less obvious such as project plans, specifications, designs and metrics [Ludewig, 2003].

In order to distinguish models from other artefacts, specific criteria are needed. According to Stachowiak's Model Theory, any candidate must fulfil three criteria being a model [Stachowiak, 1973]:

- *Mapping criterion:* there is an original object or phenomenon that is mapped to the model. This original object or phenomenon is referred to as "the original".

- *Reduction criterion:* not all the properties of the original are mapped on to the model, but the model is somehow reduced. On the other hand, the model must mirror at least some properties of the original.

- *Pragmatic criterion:* the model can replace the original for some purpose, i.e. the model is useful.

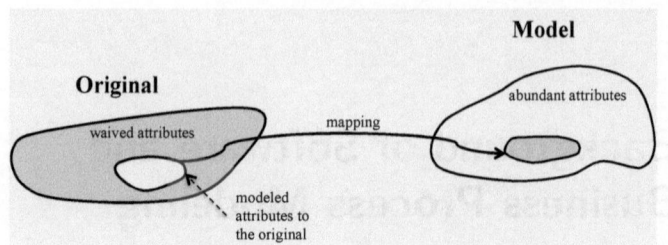

Figure 2.1.1.: Original and Model according to Stachowiak (1973)

The *mapping criterion* does not imply the actual existence of the original; it may be planned, suspected, or fictitious. The cost estimation of a software project is a speculative model of the future. A model may act as the original of another model. A program design is a model of the code to be written, while the code is a model of the computation performed by the computer when the code is executed.

At first glance, the *reduction criterion* seems to describe a weakness of models, because something is lost in the model that was present in the original. But that loss is the real strength of models: very often, the model can be handled while the original cannot.

Additionally, the *pragmatic criterion* is the reason models are applied. Since it is not possible to use the original, the model is used instead.

As an effect of the reduction, many features of the original (the waived attributes) are not found in the model. For example, the name of a person is not visible in his photograph. On the other hand, features that do not stem from the original are added (abundant attributes). For example, the size of the picture does not tell anything about the person.

Figure 2.1.1 shows the resulting relation between a original real-world domain and its associated model.

However, a weakness of Stachowiak's concept of a model is that it implies an epistemological position of positivism. This is criticized in Schuette & Rotthowe (1998), where the authors propose an alternative position based on insights from critical realism and constructivism. This position regards a model as a "result of a construct done by a modeler" [Schuette and Rotthowe, 1998].

Consequently, a relationship between a model and the modeler exists leading to limitations of resulting models, which depend on the modeler's subjective view of modeling and the domain modeled [Krogstie, 2003].

As such, it is heavily influenced by the subjective perception of the modeler. This makes modeling a non-deterministic task that requires standards in order to achieve a certain level of inter-subjectivity.

A **graphical modeling language** meets this demand for standardization in the domain of software and business process modeling.

2.2. History of Conceptual Modeling

Conceptual modeling plays an important role in the development of software applications. Modeling acts as a starting point for understanding the common basis for developers and users. Conceptual modeling integrates domain experts, who are involved in a business process, and their knowledge, into the software development.

In the following chapter a brief history of conceptual modeling is proposed starting with the roots in the early 70ies and ending with the object oriented development and related modeling languages.

The Beginning of conceptual modeling in the early 1970ies

One of the first approaches to abstraction applied to software engineering can be found in [Parnas, 1972].

The major goal of this approach is to provide precise and complete application specifications leading to the fact that other pieces of software can be developed to interact withthe application without additional information. This is achieved by providing concepts for data abstraction and hiding implementation details from the user.

Codd (1970) separated logical data organization from physical organization. This approach laid the ground for conceptual modeling and for capturing the semantics of an application [Codd, 1970].

Another important approach in the field of modeling was the programming language Simula. Simula introduced new concepts like objects, classes, methods and especially subclasses, which support the notion of generalization abstraction. Simula is considered the first object-oriented programming language and became a cornerstone of most object-oriented techniques [Dahl and Nygaard, 1966].

Conceptual modeling and Semantic Data Models in the mid 1970s

Most approaches to database design relied on modeling data structures, which are used to store the model in file systems. Two approaches are the hierarchical and the network models, both focusing on the physical level what nowadays may be called graph models [Angles and Guteierrez, 2008].

Techniques for knowledge integration as well as data abstraction were introduced by Abrial (1974). He proposed a definition of the semantics of classes by access procedures [Abrial, 1974].

Because of its simplicity, Chen's Entity-Relationship Diagram became popular and the de facto standard in data modeling and database design [Chen, 1976].

Semantic data models allow for designing models at a higher level and enable the database practitioners to naturally and directly incorporate in the schema a larger portion of the semantics of the data [Hammer and McLeod, 1978].

The Structured Analysis and Design Technique (SADT), introduced by Ross (1977) in the mid seventies, was one of the most significant early steps in the area of requirements specifications [Ross, 1977]. Among the features is the emphasis on modeling data as well as activities connected by edges representing the flow of information.

Smith and Smith (1977) have introduced concepts for abstraction and generalization in database design in database research. They combined 'generalization' and 'aggregation' into one structuring discipline. However, aggregation was still not easily modeled using ER; it became the main thrust in Object Oriented databases. The advantage of aggregation is that it provides an easier understanding of complex models and a more systematic approach to database design. It mainly supports the development of highly structured models without loss in intellectual manageability [Smith and Smith, 1977].

The first high level data definition languages for defining conceptual schemas such as the Conceptual Schema Language were discussed in the late seventies. Descriptive elements as well as procedural elements are provided within this language.

Hence, static aspects and dynamic behavior of data could be described by providing standard types, object types and association types. A prominent example of a database design language covering the concepts is Taxis [Mylopoulos et al., 1978]. Taxis provides relational database management facilities, means of specifying semantic integrity constraints incorporated into transactions, and an exception-handling mechanism. Taxis applies the concepts of class, property and generalization relationship to all aspects of program design.

An Efflorescence of conceptual modeling languages in the 1980s

The specialization has increased over the years and more and more sub-disciplines within conceptual modeling emerged. The differences between those sub-disciplines seem to arise from issues concerning notation and basic vocabulary. Only in a minority of cases, the ways to utilise the models or the ways the models are constructed justify this development.

In the domain of requirements engineering, Greenspan et al. (1994) adopted the approach of Taxis and attempted to formalize the SADT notation [Greenspan et al., 1994]. The Requirements Modeling Language embodies a notation for requirements modeling which combines object-orientation and organization, with an assertional sublanguage used to specify constraints and deductive rules [Roussopoulos and Yeh, 1984].

The Semantic Database Design takes not only the environment of the data processing system into account, but also focuses on the environment of the entire company. This approach proceeds on the assumption that without a complete understanding of how the enterprise operates, it is not possible to develop an effective design. Thus, it is recommended to start with an environment analysis phase followed by a system analysis phase, capturing and analyzing the operational behavior of an organisation.

Object-oriented development in the 1990s

In the early 1990s the term process became a new productivity paradigm. Companies were encouraged to think in processes instead of functions and procedures. The Event Driven Process Chain (EPC) notation offers many ways for modeling processes, analyzing them, and identifying improvement potentials. EPCs were invented back in 1992 by Prof. Scheer and colleagues at the University of Saarland. Since then, they have seen an industry wide adoption. EPCs are used in many industries and are supported by different modeling tools.

Furthermore, a variety of object-oriented analysis techniques has been developed in the early nineties. Important representatives of these techniques are the 'Booch Method' and Rumbaugh's 'Object modeling Technique', both offering a more coherent modeling framework than the combined use of data flow and Entity-Relationship diagrams. The Booch Method focused mainly on object-oriented design, whereas the object-modeling technique focused on object-oriented analysis.

In 1994 Booch and Rumbaugh decided to combine and unify their object-oriented modeling methods by developing the Unified modeling Language (UML) - a language for modeling object systems [OMG, 2011c].

Through the standardization efforts undertaken by the Object Management Group (OMG), UML has been rapidly adopted as a standard for modeling a very wide range of applications and domains [Booch et al., 1998].

It is claimed that one important advantage of UML is that it could be used both for modeling software and for modeling the problem domain that is supported by a system [Evermann and Wand, 2005].

By the end of the nineties it was widely agreed that information systems need to better match their operational organizational environment. Hence, requirement specification needs to cover not only software specifications but also business models and other kinds of information in describing the context in which the intended system will function. The above UML emphasizes concepts for modeling and analysis during the later requirements phases, which usually focus on completeness, consistency, and automated verification of functional requirements.

With Tropos, a development method supporting the early phases of requirement engineering is provided. Tropos is founded on the idea of using the agent paradigm and related mentalistic notions during all phases of the development software process [Bresciani et al., 2004].

2.3. Terms and Definitions in the Modeling Domain

This chapter focuses on the introduction of terms and definitions in the modeling domain. The generic term in the domain of graphical modeling languages is modeling method. Modeling methods provide the necessary concepts capable to capture relevant domain knowledge in terms of models that describe relevant aspects of the application domain. modeling methods consist of two basic components [Atkinson and Kuhne, 2003]:

- a *modeling technique*, which is divided in a modeling language and a modeling procedure

- *mechanisms* and *algorithms* working on the models described by the modeling language

The *modeling language* contains the elements, with which a model can be described. The *modeling procedure* describes the steps applying the modeling language to develop models.

A graphical modeling language is described by *syntax, semantics* and *a notation*. The syntax describes the elements and rules for creating models and is based on a grammar. The semantics describes the meaning of a modeling language and consists of a semantic domain and a semantic mapping. The semantic domain describes the meaning by using ontologies and mathematical expressions etc. The semantic mapping connects the syntactical constructs with their meaning defined in the semantic domain, i.e. semantic schema. For the formalization of semantic definitions, denotational semantics, operational semantics, axiomatic semantics or algebraic semantics are used [Petre, 2006].

The *notation* describes the visualization of the modeling language. Static approaches define the geometric shapes for visualizing the syntactical constructs, but they do not consider the state of the modeling constructs during modeling. Dynamic approaches consider the model state by splitting the notation in a representation part and a control part. The representation part maps to the static approach. The control part defines rules to query the model state and to influence the representation depending on the particular model state [Karagiannis and Kühn, 2002].

Generally, a model is developed by using a *modeling tool*. The tool represents the modeling language and may represent a modeling technique or a modeling method. A model describes a system or a system component such as application systems or business processes.

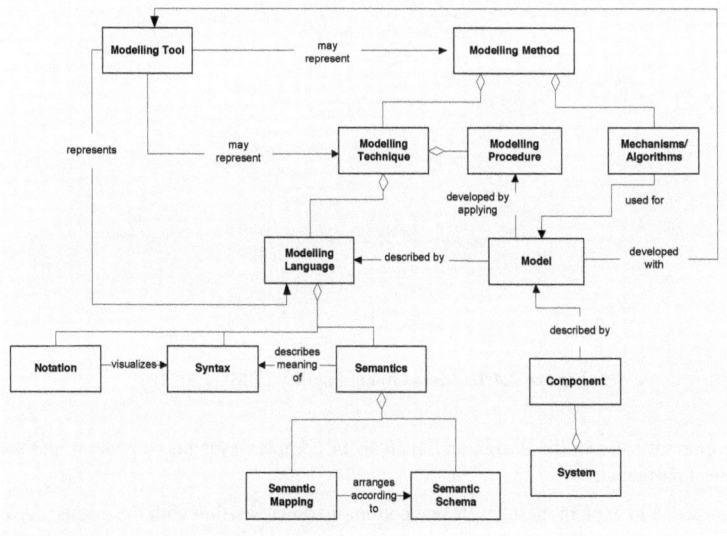

Figure 2.3.1.: Terminology of the modeling domain

The following figure was developed under consideration of Karagiannis & Kühn (2002) and shows specific terms and their relations in the domain of graphical modeling languages:

2.4. Abstraction Layers

To capture the complexity in software and business process modeling, different abstraction concepts are introduced. A traditional abstraction concept in computer science is the separation of modeling levels, from instance level to model level to metamodel level, denoted by horizontal abstraction.

For example, along the lines of the levels of abstraction identified by the OMG,

- the metamodel level,
- the model level,
- and the instance level

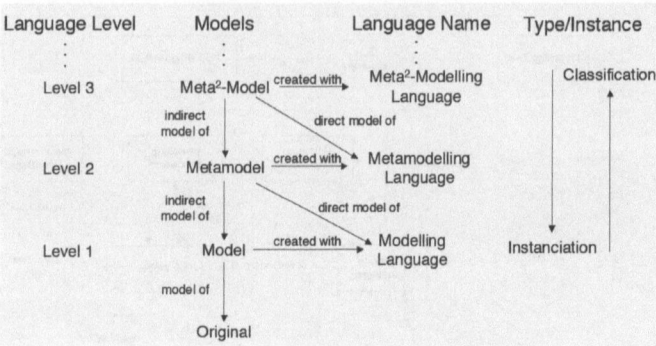

Figure 2.4.1.: Meta Object Facility [OMG, 2011b]

play important roles in the design and analysis of complex systems in general and software systems in particular.

It is instructive to explain these levels in a bottom-up order, starting with the instance level. The instance level reflects the concrete entities that are involved in business processes or applications. Executed activities, concrete data values, and resources and persons are represented at the instance level. To organize the complexity of the real-world scenarios, a set of similar entities at the instance level are identified and classified at the model level.

For instance, a set of similar business process instances are classified and represented by a business process model. In object modeling, a set of similar entities is represented by a class, and in data modeling using the Entity Relationship approach, a set of similar entities is represented by an entity type, and similar relationships between entity types are represented by a relationship type.

2.5. Modeling in Software Engineering

In the field of Software Engineering modeling became popular with Peter Chen's Entity-Relationship Diagram [Chen, 1976].

Since object orientation has evolved in the early 1990ies, modeling has become a self-contained and growing area in the domain of Software Engineering. Following the wide dissemination of the UML, the Model Driven Development and Model Driven Architecture approach has moved modeling into the centre of the software development process.

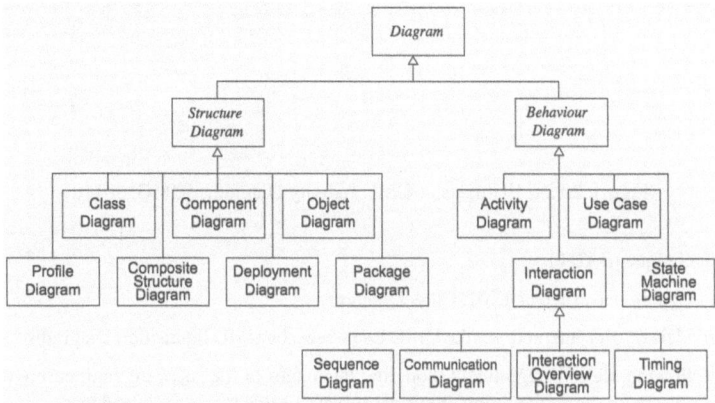

Figure 2.5.1.: The UML 2.0 Diagram Types [OMG, 2011c]

In this thesis, the UML in the version 2.0 plays a significant role due to its current ubiquity in the domain of software engineering. The UML is a standardized modeling language in the field of object-oriented software engineering. The standard was created and is managed by the OMG.

UML includes a set of graphic notation techniques to create visual models of object-oriented software-intensive systems. UML diagrams represent two different types of a system model [OMG, 2011c]:

- **Static or structural models:** emphasizes the static structure of the system using objects, attributes, operations and relationships. The structural view includes class diagrams and composite structure diagrams.

- **Dynamic or behavioral models:** emphasizes the dynamic behavior of the system by showing collaborations among objects and changes to the internal states of objects. This view includes sequence diagrams, activity diagrams and state machine diagrams.

The following figure shows an overall view of the diagrams of the UML:

Models can be found in all areas and applications of software engineering. While software developers create concrete models people who do research in software engineering work on notations and methods for developing such concrete models. Class Diagrams and State Charts, Petri Nets and Data Flow Diagrams are a few examples of models that use such notations. Most of the models used in software engineering are prescriptive, for instance:

- process models, such as UML Activity Diagrams

- information flow models such as the diagrams used in structured Analysis and Design

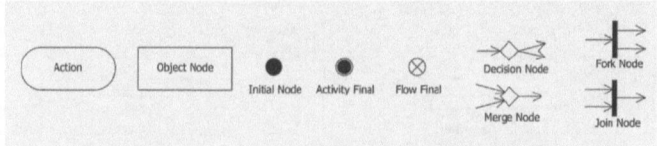

Figure 2.5.2.: Elements of UML Activity Diagrams [OMG, 2011d]

Technique (SADT)

- design models, such as UML Class Diagrams,
- models of user interaction, like UML Use Cases, or UML Interaction Diagrams

In the following sections significant modeling languages of the software engineering domain that are relevant in the forthcoming empirical surveys of this thesis are introduced.

2.5.1. UML 2.0 Activity Diagrams

The UML 2.0 Activity Diagram belongs to the behavioral diagrams of the UML and was designed for modeling processes and flows in application systems [OMG, 2011c].

The diagram is approximated on Petri Nets, and uses also the notion of token. Main concepts of the Activity Diagram are actions and activity partitions.

An activity partition is used to group actions executed by a certain role.

The main elements of a UML Activity Diagram is the *activity* and different *activity nodes. Action, object node and control node* are a specialization of an *activity node.*

Action describes the atomic task of an Activity Diagram. An *object node* is an activity node that indicates an instance of a particular classifier, possibly in a particular state, may be available at a particular point in the activity [OMG, 2011d].

Control nodes define the behavior of an Activity Diagram.

The *initial node* starts the activity. If an activity contains more *initial nodes*, different flows are executed concurrently.

The *final node* is split up into *activity final node* and *flow final node*. While the *activity final node* terminates all flows within an activity, the *flow final node* only terminates one flow, and the *activity* is unaffected.

The *fork node* splits the flow into concurrent paths. A *fork node* has one incoming flow and two ore more outgoing flows. A *join node* has two or more incoming flows and one outgoing flow.

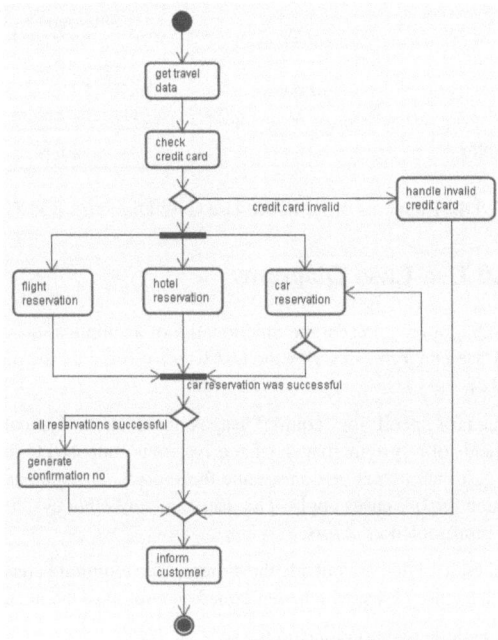

Figure 2.5.3.: Example Model of an UML 2.0 Activity Diagram

A *decision node* has one incoming flow and several outgoing flows. A *decision node* splits up into several alternative flows. Only one outgoing flow will be chosen for further processing.

The *merge node* merges the outgoing flows of the *decision node*. A merge node brings multiple alternate flows together.

In an activity the flow of control form one node to another is modeled using *control flow* edges and *data flow* edges.

The *control flow* models the flow between *actions*, and the *data flow* between *object nodes* and *actions*.

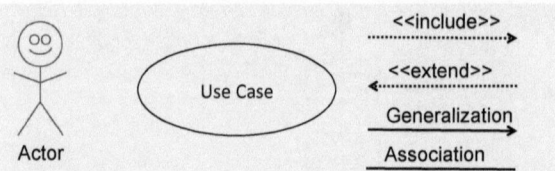

Figure 2.5.4.: Elements of UML 2.0 Use Case Diagrams [OMG, 2011d]

2.5.2. UML 2.0 Use Case Diagrams

UML 2.0 Use Case Diagrams represent the functionality of an application system from a user's point of view. Use Case Diagrams describe the Use Cases offered by the particular application system [OMG, 2011d].

Use cases are a means for specifying required usages of a system. Typically, they are used to capture the requirements of a system, that is, what a system is supposed to do. The key concepts associated with use cases are *actors*, *use cases*, and the *subject*. The *subject* is the system under consideration to which the use cases apply. The users and any other systems that may interact with the subject are represented as *actors*.

Actors always model entities that are outside the system. The required behavior of the subject is specified by one or more use cases, which are defined according to the needs of actors.

Use Case Diagrams include two relationship types:

- A use case may include another use case. *Include* is a directed relationship between two use cases, implying that the behavior of the included use case is inserted into the behavior of the including use case.

- A use case may *extend* another use case. The relationship indicates that the behavior of the extension use case may be inserted in the extended use case.

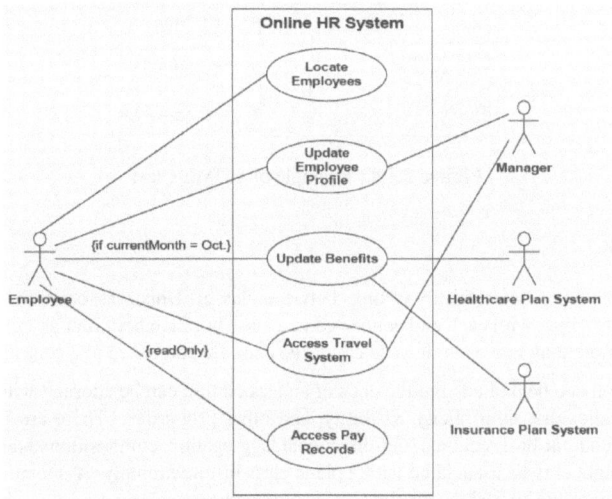

Figure 2.5.5.: Example of a UML 2.0 Use Case Diagram

2.5.3. UML 2.0 Class Diagrams

The Class Diagram is a static structure diagram of the UML and describes a system by showing the system's classes, their attributes, operations and the relationship among the classes [OMG, 2011d]. Class Diagrams are used to

- explore domain concepts in the form of a domain model,
- analyze requirements in the form of a conceptual model,
- depict the detailed design of object-oriented systems [Ambler, 2005].

The elements of UML Class Diagrams consist of

- *Classes* including a *classname, attributes* and *operations*
- Relations including *association, aggregation, composition* and *generalization*

A *class* is an object oriented system that provides a crisp abstraction of a well defined set of responsibilities. The relationships for classes are logical connections between classes. The UML 2.0 shows the following basic relationships [OMG, 2011d]:

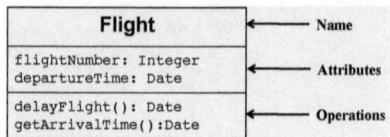

Figure 2.5.6.: Example of a UML Class

Association:

An association represents a family of links between classes. Binary associations are normally represented as a line, with each end connected to a class box. Higher order associations can be drawn with more than two ends. In such cases, the ends are connected to a central diamond.

An association can be named, and the ends of an association can be adorned with role names, ownership indicators, multiplicity, visibility, and other properties. There are four different types of association: bi-directional, uni-directional, aggregation, composition and reflexive. For instance, a flight class is associated with a plane class bi-directionally. Association represents the static relationship shared among the objects of two classes.

Aggregation:

An aggregation is related to the "has a" or association relationship. An aggregation is more specific than an association. It is an association that represents a part-whole or part-of relationship. As a type of association, an aggregation can be named and have the same adornments that an association can. However, an aggregation may not involve more than two classes.

Composition:

A composition is a stronger variant of the "owns a" or association relationship. A composition is more specific than an aggregation. A composition has a strong life cycle dependency between instances of the container class and instances of the contained class: If the container is destroyed, normally every instance that it contains is destroyed as well.

Generalization:

The generalization relationship indicates that one of the two related classes i.e. the subclass is considered to be a specialized form of the other class and is considered as 'generalization' of the subclass. This means that any instance of the subtype is also an instance of the superclass. An

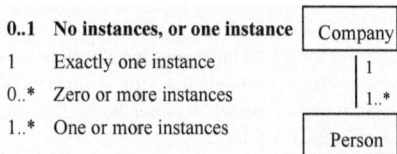

Figure 2.5.7.: Multiplicities in UML 2.0 Class Diagrams [OMG, 2011c]

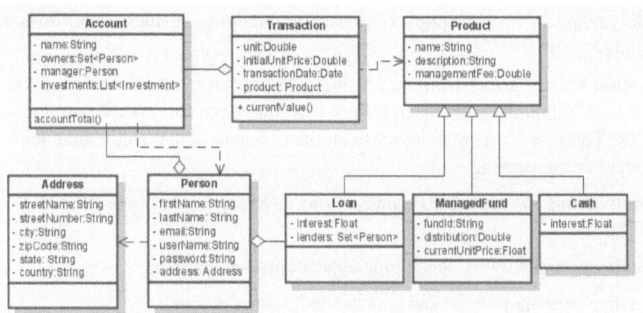

Figure 2.5.8.: Example of a UML 2.0 Class Diagram

exemplary tree of generalizations of this form is found in binomial nomenclature: human beings are a subclass of simian, which are a subclass of mammal etc. The relationship is most easily understood by the phrase 'an A is a B'.

Multiplicity:

The association relationship indicates that one of the two related classes makes reference to the other. In contrast with the generalization relationship, this is most easily understood through the phrase 'A has a B', for example a building has one or more rooms, an employee belongs to one company.

2.6. Business Process Modeling

Over the past decades, the modeling of business processes has become an indispensable means of conceptualizing and designing business organizations and the subsequent engineering of appropriate IT-support.

Since over time various different modeling languages have been developed, as a result differing legacy models exist. Business Process Models describe sequences of activities, expressed in a certain modeling language, with the model elements being labelled following the business terminology in use in the applicable domain.

One of the core tasks in business management is the design and continuous improvement of business processing according to changing needs and expectations and the allocation of all necessary resources. The increasing speed of globalization demands from enterprises of all sizes to adequately adapt in an ever quickening pace to changing business conditions and varying market requirements.

The motivation mostly arises from increasing cost pressure and intensifying competition as well as new legal regulations, the need to follow standards or for incorporating new innovative technologies. Therefore, it is mandatory to engineer business in an agile manner for on-going optimization or reengineering.

Possible motivations for applying Business Process Modeling in organizations are defined by Havey (2005):

- Reducing complexity by developing abstract process models
- Formalize existing process and spot needed improvements
- Facilitate automated, efficient process flow
- Increase productivity and decrease head count
- Simplify regulations and compliance issues [Havey, 2005]

In the following sections significant modeling languages of the business process modeling domain that are relevant in the empirical surveys of this thesis are introduced.

2.6.1. Event Driven Process Chains

Event Driven Process Chains have been developed within the framework of the Architecture of Integrated Information Systems (ARIS). EPCs are used by many companies for modeling, analyzing and redesigning business processes. EPCs are the key component of SAP R/3s[1] modeling concepts for business engineering and customizing.

EPCs are based on the concepts of Stochastic Networks and Petri Nets. They are a graphical business process description language. They describe business processes on the level of their business logic and are targeted to be easy understood and used by business people. The denotation represents the control flow structure of the process as a chain of events and functions [Scheer, 1992].

---

[1]www.sap.com

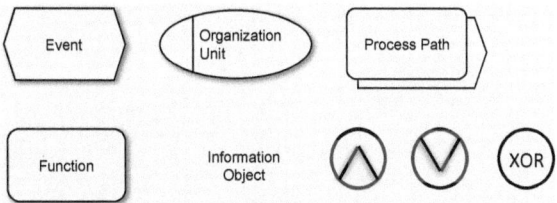

Figure 2.6.1.: Elements of EPCs

EPCs consist of the following elements [Scheer, 1992]:

1. *Functions* are active element and represent the activities.

2. *Events* are created by processing functions or by actors. An Event acts as a pre-condition of a function or corresponds to the post-condition of another one.

3. *Logical operators* connect functions and events. Three types of logical operators exist: *AND, XOR* (exclusive or) and *OR*.

4. The *organization unit* is responsible for performing an activity or a function.

5. *Information objects* represent input data serving as a basis for a function, or output data produced by a function. They correspond to entities of the Entity-Relationship Model.

6. The *process path* element serves as navigation aid in the EPC. They show the connection from or to other processes.

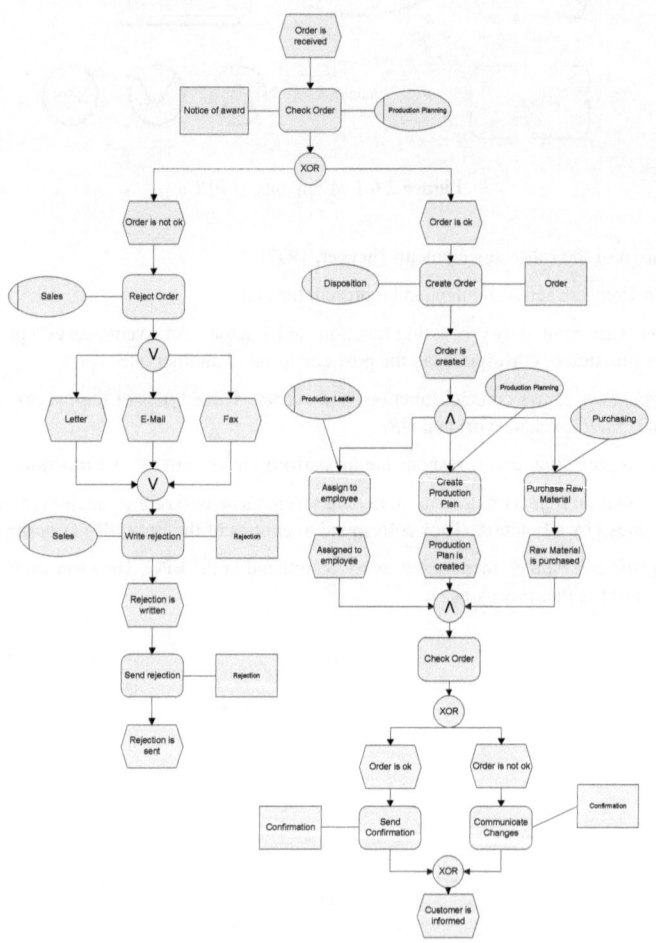

Figure 2.6.2.: Example EPC Diagram

Core Set of BPMN Elements

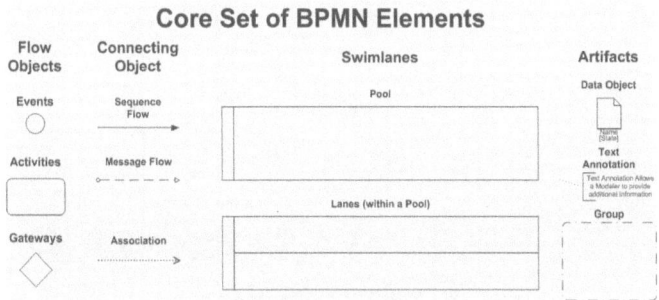

Figure 2.6.3.: Core Elements of the BPMN 2.0 [OMG, 2011a]

2.6.2. Business Process Modeling Notation 2.0 (BPMN)

The Business Process Modeling Notation (BPMN) is a standard notation for capturing business processes, especially at the level of domain analysis and high-level systems design. BPMN was developed by Business Process Management Initiative, and is currently maintained by the Object Management Group. As of March 2011, the current version of BPMN is 2.0. The notation inherits and combines elements from a number of previously proposed notations for business process modeling, including the XML Process Definition Language (XPDL) and the Activity Diagrams component of the UML. BPMN process models are composed of [OMG, 2011a]:

- *activity nodes,* denoting *business events* or items of work performed by humans or by software applications and

- *control nodes* capturing the flow of control between activities.

Activity nodes and control nodes can be connected by means of a flow relation in almost arbitrary ways. The BPMN consist currently of 116 different elements in the version 2.0. The following figure shows the core elements of the BPMN. A full set of elements can be found in the appendix of this thesis.

BPMN is also supported with appropriate graphical object properties that will enable the generation of executable Business Process Execution Language (BPEL). Thus, BPMN creates a standardized bridge for the gap between the business process design and process implementation. However, a variety of limitations of BPMN such as construct deficits, redundancy and construct overload were analyzed [Recker et al., 2006].

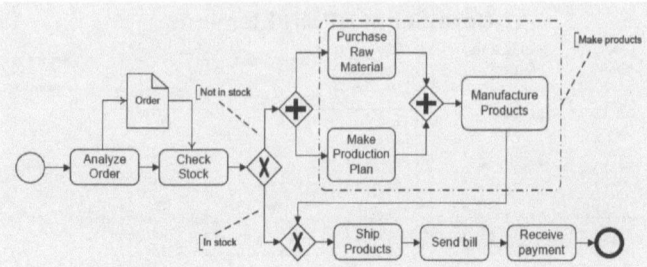

Figure 2.6.4.: Example BPMN 2.0 Diagram

2.7. Similarities between different Modeling Concepts

The general aim of the empirical study presented in this thesis is the conduction of a usability survey focusing on graphical modeling languages in general. As shown in the chapters above several concepts of modeling do exist. The question that has to be answered is whether parallels between the different modeling concepts do exist or not. Therefore, the body of graphical modeling languages is analyzed and consequently parallels between different modeling concepts are defined.

A graphical modeling language consists of a set of graphical shapes (visual vocabulary), a set of compositional rules (visual grammar) and definitions of the meaning of each symbol (visual semantics).

The visual vocabulary and visual grammar together form the visual (or concrete) syntax. Graphical symbols are used to symbolize (perceptually represent) semantic constructs, typically defined by a metamodel [Moody and Heymans, 2010].

The meanings of graphical symbols are defined by mapping them to the constructs they represent. A valid expression in a visual notation is called a visual sentence or diagram. Diagrams are composed of symbol instances (tokens), arranged according to the rules of the visual grammar.

Figure 2.7.1 summarizes the previous section and shows the relationships between the instance and the metalevel of graphical modeling languages. The metalevel of a graphical modeling language can be defined as metamodel of the language regulating the syntax and the different elements. The instance level denotes the concrete level, i.e. the concrete model that consists of concrete shapes and semantic constructs.

Due to the fact, that the following survey aims to be a cross-language survey over different modeling concepts the similarities of different modeling concepts and consequently the similarity of resulting languages has to be defined.

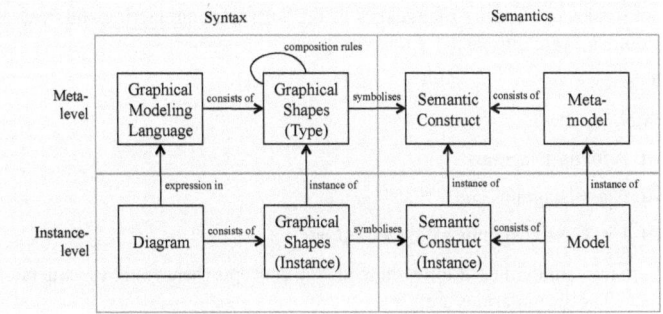

Figure 2.7.1.: Anatomy of graphical modeling Languages

Referring to Moody (2010) it can be concluded that the survey is influenced by the metalevel and the instance level of modeling languages. The metalevel (i.e. the metamodel) contains the graphical shapes, the relationships, semantics and the syntax.

This language-specific level influences the usability of graphical modeling languages. In other words, two relevant components of the metamodel can be extracted:

- Visual Syntax (Language Complexity)
- Graphical Shapes (Visual Properties)

On the other hand, the instance level is important as well. For testing the usability with individuals in a survey it is necessary to confront them with concrete models/diagrams of particular languages. Consequently, the influence of those concrete models/diagrams has to be considered and the data material has to be adjusted. For this, a specific algorithm is developed and introduced in chapter 5 of this thesis.

2.8. Chapter Conclusion

This chapter presented the conceptual background of software and process modeling including the history of graphical modeling as well as terms and definitions in the modeling domain. According to Stachowiak's Model Theory, any model must fulfil three criteria being a model [Stachowiak, 1973]:

- Mapping criterion
- Reduction criterion
- Pragmatic criterion

Furthermore, relevant modeling languages of the software engineering and business process modeling domain were introduced. Concerning this,

- EPC's,

- BPMN,

- UML Activity Diagrams,

- UML Class Diagrams and

- UML Use Case Diagrams were focused on.

In addition to this, similarities of different modeling concepts (behavioral vs. structural concepts) were defined. Those similarities are:

- metalevel including shapes, relations, semantics and syntax

- instance level including concrete models/diagrams

This definition is important since the following survey aims to be a cross-language survey over different modeling concepts. In general, this chapter shows the theoretical basis of this thesis concerning the used terms and languages.

3. Background Theories

In this chapter the theoretical background of the study conducted in this thesis is developed. Usability theory has its roots in cognitive psychology and is a relatively young branch of computer science. A common understanding of the theoretical factors influencing usability and their interrelations is currently not existing. Therefore, the theoretical context for this thesis consists of several parts of strong theories, which are introduced in the following chapter. Those theories are necessary for the surveys conducted in this thesis and are applied in Part III of this thesis.

3.1. Communication Theory

In general, the presented theory is an adaptation of Shannon and Weaver's widely accepted theory of communication [Shannon et al., 1998]. It was applied to visual notations i.e. graphical modeling languages by Daniel L. Moody [Moody, 2009].

As shown in Figure 3.1.1, a model developer (sender) encodes information (message) in the form of a model (signal) and the diagram user (receiver) decodes this signal.

The diagram is encoded using a graphical modeling language (code), which defines a set of conventions that both sender and receiver understand. The medium (channel) is the physical form in which the model is presented (e.g., paper, whiteboard, and computer screen).

Noise represents random variation in the signal, which can interfere with communication. The effectiveness of communication is measured by the match between the intended message and the received message (information transmitted). In this theory, communication consists of two complementary processes: encoding (expression) and decoding (interpretation).

To optimize communication, it is essential to consider both [Moody, 2009]:

Encoding: What are the available options for encoding information in visual form? This defines the design space: the set of possible graphic encodings for a given message, which is virtually unlimited [Bertin, 1983].

Decoding: How are graphical modeling languages processed by the human mind? This defines the solution space: principles of human information processing provide the basis for choosing among the infinite possibilities in the design space [Moody, 2009].

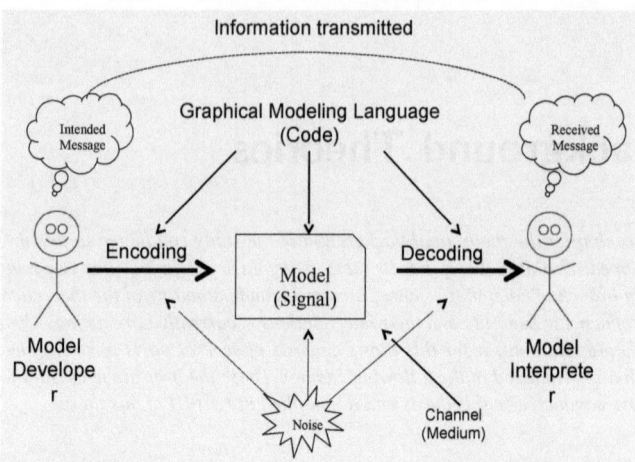

Figure 3.1.1.: Communication Theory and Modeling Languages

Relevance for the Empirical Studies of this Thesis

The presented Communication Theory is relevant for the empirical surveys conducted in this thesis due to the fact that modeling in enterprises is strongly connected to encoding and decoding information.

For example, a software engineer encodes information such as use cases, classes or activities in specific diagrams of the UML. Based on those diagrams a software developer decodes the information modelled and develops a program code.

Thus, modeling languages support to decode and encode relevant information about a system or a business process in enterprises.

Consequently, the presented Communication Theory has to be considered in a survey on usability evaluation of graphical modeling languages.

3.2. Activity Theory

Origins of Activity Theory can be traced to the classical german philosophy of Kant, Hegel and Fichte. However, Activity Theory is today mostly associated with Lev Vygotsky and the cultural-historical school of Russian psychologists, who explored objective, ecological, and socio-cultural perspectives of activity-based philosophy of Marx and Engels [Kuutti, 1995].

In addition, Activity Theory has parallels with a number of Anglo-American traditions, such as Dewey's pragmatism and Mead's symbolic interactionism [Kuutti, 1995].

Activity Theory is founded on a number of interrelated basic concepts and principles that constitute a general conceptual system or framework. In the following the basic key concepts of activity theory are summarized and transferred in the domain of graphical modeling languages.

Object Orientedness

Activity Theory includes a subject, which refers to the individual or sub-group whose agency is chosen as the point of view in the analysis. The object refers to the raw material or problem space at which the activity is directed and which is modelled and transformed into outcomes with the help of physical and symbolic, external and internal mediating instruments, including both tools and signs. Transferring this to the domain of graphical modeling languages leads to the fact that

- a subject is characterized by the user of graphical modeling languages whereas
- the object can be defined as graphical model/diagram.

Hierarchy

Leontjev (1978) proposes that an activity has a hierarchical structure with three distinct levels:

- the activity level,
- the action level and
- the operation level [Leontiev, 1978].

Activities consist of actions, which consist of operations. Actions are basic components of activities. Different actions may be undertaken to meet the same goal. Operations are ways of executing actions, and represent the concrete conditions required to achieve goals.

In the domain of graphical modeling languages an

- activity can occur as model development task,
- a possible action may be encoding or decoding of information to be developed or interpreted and
- a possible operation may be the handling of a modeling tool.

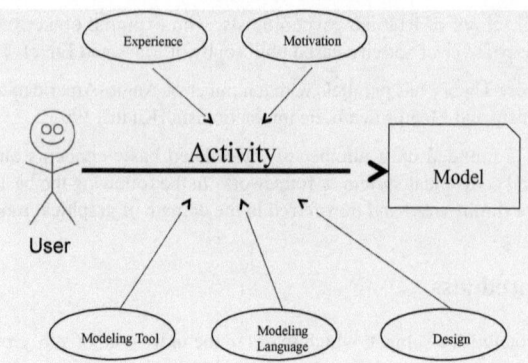

Figure 3.2.1.: Activity Theory in the Domain of graphical Modeling Languages

Mediation

Activity Theory emphasizes that human activity is mediated by artefacts. The mediating artifact can be external (e.g. modeling tool) or internal (e.g. motivation, modeling experience).

Figure 3.2.1 subsumes the concepts of Activity Theory and shows the adoption of this theory on graphical modeling languages.

Relevance for the Empirical Studies of this Thesis

Usability research builds up on the concepts of Activity Theory [Nielsen, 2006b]. The activity in the domain of graphical modeling languages is the development or the interpretation of models.

Concerning this, the activity is mediated by several artefacts, which has to be considered in an empirical survey in this research area. Artefacts such as participant experience and motivation, the modeling tool, the modeling language and model design has to be considered as control variables in a survey focusing on usability evaluation of graphical modeling languages.

3.3. Cognitive Theories

Cognitive theories are central to the usability evaluation of different modeling languages. Mental processes as visual perception, information processing, reasoning and problem solving, attention,

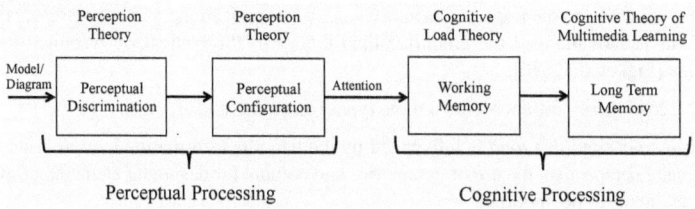

Figure 3.3.1.: Human Information Processing in the Domain of Graphical Modeling Languages

as well as short and long-term memory are affected in learning how to use specific modeling languages, creating models, and understanding models.

Figure 3.3.1 shows a model of human graphical information processing, which reflects current research in visual perception and cognition [Moody, 2009].

Processing is divided into two phases: perceptual processing (seeing) and cognitive processing (understanding). Perceptual processes are automatic, very fast, and mostly executed in parallel, while cognitive processes operate under conscious control of attention and are relatively slow, effortful, and sequential.

A major explanation for the cognitive advantages of diagrams is computational offloading: They shift some of the processing burden from the cognitive system to the perceptual system, which is faster and frees up scarce cognitive resources for other tasks. The extent to which diagrams exploit perceptual processing largely explains differences in their effectiveness [Larkin and Simon, 1987].

First, cognitive theory is underlain, which generally defines the external impact of human learning and acting. The theoretical constructs of cognitive psychology have direct analogies in model development and model interpretation scenarios. From the traditional cognitive point of view, the usability system in this study is composed of three basic units generating and processing information:

- the human being acts as model developer and model interpreter processing information,
- the model task, which provides the information and
- the modeling language, which determines the interpretation or graphical representation of given information.

3.3.1. Cognitive Load Theory

The second theory is a development of cognitive theory called cognitive load theory [Plass et al., 2010].

This theory focuses on the impact of memory load to human learning and knowledge acquisition. Figl et al. (2010) mapped the cognitive load theory to the context of graphical modeling languages [Figl et al., 2010].

Cognitive load theory differs between three types of cognitive load:

The *extraneous cognitive load* is influenced by the way the information is represented. From the language perspective, the use of geometrics and colours for designing elements of modeling languages seems to be important.

The *intrinsic cognitive load* is determined by information complexity and interaction. For example, learning elements of modeling languages results in a low intrinsic cognitive load. In this case, the difficulty of learning a language and consequently the intrinsic cognitive load is strongly connected with the range of elements a language consists of. Contrariwise, the element interaction by means of syntactical and semantic element relations leads to a high intrinsic cognitive load. Furthermore, the intrinsic cognitive load is influenced by prior knowledge of human beings [Sweller, 2005].

Considering this in the survey leads to the importance of including experience in the proposed research model in Part II of this thesis.

Finally, *germane cognitive load* is the result of beneficial cognitive processes such as abstractions and elaborations that are promoted by the instructional presentation [Sweller, 2005, Plass et al., 2010].

Relevance for the Empirical Studies of this Thesis

Cognitive Load Theory is focusing on model development and interpretation tasks. Firstly, models represent complex organizational relationships in a visual diagram. Humans have limited information processing capabilities [Plass et al., 2010].

Secondly, the complexity of a modeling language influences the process of model development by humans. Due to the fact that humans have limited capabilities processing information in the brain the Cognitive Load Theory is an important theoretical basis.

The Cognitive Load Theory focuses on the **Working Memory:** This is a temporary storage area used for active processing, which reflects the current focus of attention. It has very limited capacity and duration and is a known bottleneck in visual information processing [Lohse, 1997, Kosslyn, 1989].

Therefore, a main goal in the design of modeling languages is to reduce cognitive load for users to enable more effective problem solving i.e. development or interpretation of models. Low cognitive load is positively related to a variety of quality aspects of models, such as perceived ease of understanding [Maes and Poels, 2007].

Cognitive load is determined by the amount of elements needed to be paid attention to at a point of time.

Consequently, the concepts of this theory has to be considered in the empirical surveys of this thesis.

3.3.2. Cognitive Theory of Multimedia Learning

The Cognitive Theory of Multimedia Learning (CTML) is used to explain how individuals viewing explanative material (such as a process model) develop understanding of content being presented to them [Mayer, 1989].

This theory was chosen for several reasons:

First, it focuses on words and graphics, which in fact are elements in any graphical modeling language.

Secondly, it provides principles for the design of effective content presentations in the form of textual and/or graphical descriptions (i.e., a model) that can be tested empirically. Third, there is an established track record of experimental studies in conceptual modeling that has successfully used CTML to establish empirically observable differences in studies of conceptual modeling languages, e.g., in the data modeling domain [Bodart et al., 2001, Gemino and Wand, 2003].

CTML suggests three outcomes that are possible when presenting explanative material in the form of models:

1. no learning,

2. fragmented learning and

3. meaningful learning.

These outcomes are primarily based on measures of two variables that Mayer labels retention and transfer [Mayer, 1989]. Retention is defined as the comprehension of material being presented. Transfer, or problem solving is the ability to use knowledge gained from the material to solve related problems.

No learning occurs where comprehension and problem solving are low. Fragmented learning occurs where comprehension is high but problem solving is low. Such result indicates material has been received but has not been well integrated with prior knowledge. This suggests memorization rather than meaningful learning has occurred.

Finally, meaningful learning occurs when both comprehension and problem solving are high. High problem solving indicates information has been integrated into long-term knowledge and a high level of understanding of the presented material has been achieved.

Relevance for the Empirical Studies of this Thesis

In the context of this thesis, the CTML focuses on model development and interpretation tasks. To be understood, information from a model must be integrated with prior knowledge stored in **Long Term Memory** by learning. This is a permanent storage area that has unlimited capacity and duration but is relatively slow [Kosslyn, 1985].

Differences in prior knowledge (expert-novice differences) greatly affect speed and accuracy of interpreting models.

Furthermore, this concept may easily be projected onto development scenarios: A model developer encodes information with prior knowledge. Differences in prior knowledge greatly affect speed and accuracy of developing models.

3.3.3. Perception Theory

Theories of visual perception play an important role in the upcoming usability evaluation survey. Especially, those theories are relevant for model scenarios in which models are interpreted and the contained information is extracted and decoded by an interpreting user.

Concerning this, a model (e.g. software model or process model) can be seen as graph with nodes and edges. When humans analyze a graph, early cognitive visual processes detect and encode visual primitives such as shape, position, colour, and length [Lohse, 1993].

Subsuming the situation in literature it is possible to define three stages in human graphical information processing:

1. **Perceptual Discrimination:** Features of the retinal image (colour, shape, etc.) are detected by specialized feature detectors [Lohse, 1993, Treisman, 1982]. Based on this, the diagram is parsed into its constituent elements and separated from the background [Palmer and Rock, 1994, Winn, 2002]. In the area of graphical modeling, several languages with differing grades of perceptual discrimination exist. The most obvious characteristics of perceptual distinction are the use of various shapes and various colours for the different elements.

2. **Perceptual Configuration:** Structure and relationships among diagram elements are inferred based on their visual characteristics [Palmer and Rock, 1994, Winn, 2002]. The Gestalt Laws of Perceptual Organization define how visual stimuli are organized into patterns or structures [Wertheimer, 1938].

3. **Attention:** All or a part of the perceptually processed image is brought into working memory under conscious control of attention. Perceptual precedence determines the order in which elements are attended to [Kosslyn, 2002, Winn, 2002].

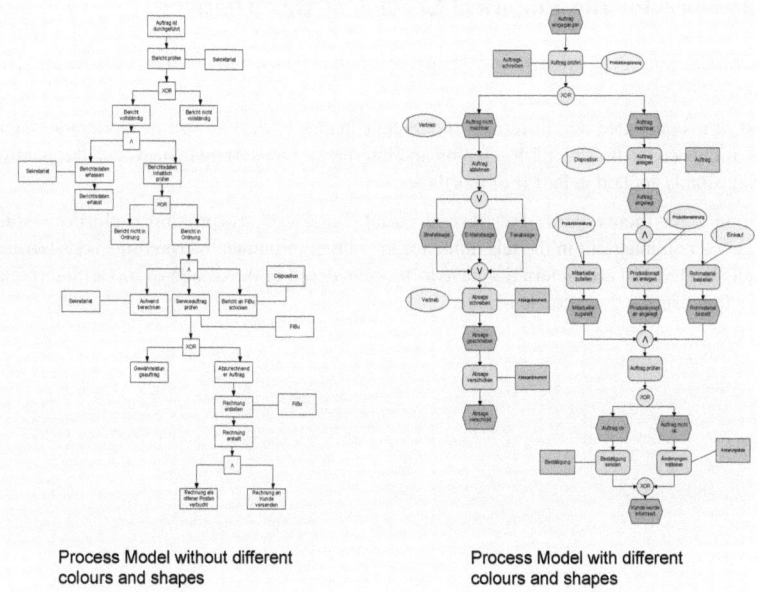

Process Model without different
colours and shapes

Process Model with different
colours and shapes

Figure 3.3.2.: Comparison of two models regarding their perceptual distinction

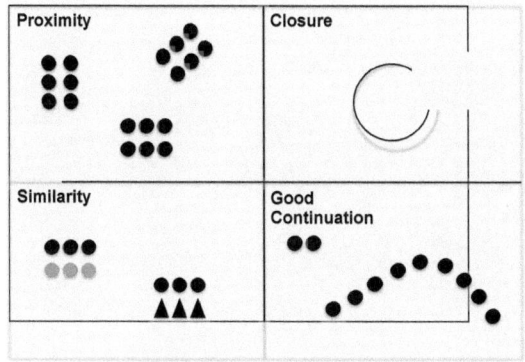

Figure 3.3.3.: The Gestalt Laws

Relevance for the Empirical Studies of this Thesis

The relevance of Perception Theory for the research conducted in this thesis is structured in two areas.

First, it is concluded that different colours and shapes of the element of modeling languages may influence the process of developing and interpreting models by humans. Consequently, this conclusion is applied in Part II of this thesis.

Secondly, the theory shows that several visual characteristics (proximity, closure, similarity and good continuation) in models influence the output of human interpreting. Transferring this means, that visual characteristics have to be considered in the design of model interpretation tasks for ensuring comparable results.

Part II.

EVALUATION FRAMEWORK AND EMPIRICAL ANALYSIS

4. A Framework for Usability Evaluation of Modeling Languages (FUEML)

This chapter includes the development of an evaluation framework focusing on the usability assessment of graphical modeling languages. Concerning this, the present status quo in research is analyzed and presented. Furthermore, an adequate definition of usability and related attributes is analyzed. Based on this, qualified metrics and measurement methods are developed for measuring the different attributes of usability in the domain of graphical modeling languages. This evaluation framework acts as a basis for the usability surveys conducted in the further course of this thesis [Schalles et al., 2010b].

In recent years, various different modeling languages and tools were developed to support the process of modeling in the field of software and business process engineering. Past usability research was not focused on modeling languages. Most usability evaluation surveys are mainly focusing on applications, websites, software and technical products. Usability has not been considered within the development of current languages for conceptual modeling such as EPCs or the diagrams of the UML.

Hence, this chapter aims to define usability in the domain of graphical modeling languages. Based on this, a usability evaluation framework for graphical modeling languages is developed [Schalles et al., 2010a]. This framework, which is called FUEML (Framework for Usability Evaluation of Modeling Languages), acts as a basis for the empirical study described in this thesis.

4.1. Usability and Modeling Languages: The Status Quo in Research

In the past many researchers have evaluated modeling languages and came up with improvements for different parts of these languages. These evaluations are based on empirical surveys as well as experienced theoretical assessments. In general, several studies for evaluating systems, modeling methods and modeling languages exist. These studies can be structured in three main categories [Siau and Rossi, 2008]:

1. Feature comparison studies

2. Theoretical and conceptual evaluation studies

3. Empirical evaluation studies

Feature Comparison Studies   Feature comparison studies are mostly based on the idea of using different languages to model the same domain and determining how various modeling languages tackle the same problem [Olle et al., 1986]. For example, within these studies the comparison of object oriented and structured development methods and process modeling methods was conducted
[Barbier and Henderson-Sellers, 2000, Loy, 1990, Strom, 1986].

Theoretical and conceptual Evaluation Studies   Theoretical and conceptual evaluation studies formalize the evaluation by developing and using frameworks and other reference disciplines such as cognitive psychology and philosophy [Bubenko, 1986].

Arnesen and Krogstie (2005) analyzed modeling languages transferring a model quality framework to their needs of language evaluation. Their framework contains a set-theoretic approach to the discussion of model quality at different semiotic levels. The associated evaluation is based on practical experiences and more theoretical evaluations of modeling languages [Arnesen and Krogstie, 2005].

According to this research, Wahl and Sindre (2005) used the semiotic quality framework for evaluating Business Process Modeling Notation (BPMN). In this evaluation study they were focusing on semantic, syntactical and pragmatic aspects of the different signs in BPMN [Wahl and Sindre, 2005].

Siau and Wang (2007) evaluated information modeling methods such as Use Case Diagrams, Rich Picture Diagrams and Entity Relationship Diagrams with applying a list of critical questions for evaluating knowledge representation. This study was based on practical experiences and theoretical evaluations. They concluded that empirical studies e.g. case study, experiment or survey would be a good follow up to this study for completing and extending the results and analysis [Siau and Wang, 2007].

Bobkowska (2005) developed a methodological framework for evaluating visual i.e. graphical modeling languages [Bobkowska, 2005a].

Dumas et al. (2005) developed a pattern-based framework to evaluate the control-flow, the data and the resource perspective of BPMN [Dumas et al., 2005].

Eloranta et al. (2006) analyzed the two modeling languages BPMN and UML. The evaluation was based on different frameworks known as the Workflow Patterns Framework and the Bunge-Weber-Wand Model (BWW-model) [Eloranta et al., 2006].

Empirical Evaluation Studies   Empirical evaluation studies target observations and propositions based on sense experience with considering methods of inductive logic including mathematics and statistics [Cooper and Schindler, 2005].

Recker and Dreiling (2007) conducted a survey on understanding process modeling languages including EPC's and BPMN. They dealt with the investigation of how learning affects modeling works. Particularly, this empirical study focuses the interpretation of diagrams developed with EPC's and BPMN and comes up with the result that process modelers with training in any process modeling language perform reasonably well in understanding other unknown process models [Recker and Dreiling, 2007].

Mendling and Strembeck (2008) analyzed influence factors of understanding business process models with applying an online questionnaire [Mendling and Strembeck, 2008]. The results of this survey support the hypothesis that personal, model and content related factors influence the understandability of process models. As the analyzed related work has shown, previous studies are mainly evaluating partitions of usability regarding modeling languages.

Siau and Rossi (2007) concluded a lack of empirical evaluation considering practical scenarios. Furthermore they strongly propose further surveys to study the usability of modeling languages [Siau and Rossi, 2008].

Mendling and Strembeck (2008) recommend future surveys for analyzing the understandability of process models [Mendling and Strembeck, 2008].

Overhage and Schlauderer (2010) compared the usability of BPMN and UML Activity diagrams based on the Bunge-Weber-Wand Ontology [Birkmeier et al., 2010].

The results of this literature research suggest current research activities in the field of user-oriented assessment of graphical modeling languages. Furthermore, they show a current research need for an overall survey evaluating the usability of graphical modeling languages. Thus, the usability evaluation framework associated with graphical modeling languages presented in this chapter is the first step to study usability in the domain of graphical modeling languages.

4.2. Usability Attributes for Modeling Languages

Defining usability in the domain of graphical modeling languages means to find suitable usability attributes for this domain. However, the aim is to hold the number of attributes as small as possible preventing semantic redundancy of them. Consequently, current usability definitions appearing in literature and standards have to be analyzed. This procedure builds up a basis for defining usability in the domain of graphical modeling languages. Subsequently, different attributes are operationalized by defining specific metrics for the domain of graphical modeling languages.

4.2.1. Heterogeneous Usability Definitions

Usability has not been defined homogeneously yet, neither by researchers nor by standardization organizations. The variety of definitions and measurement models of usability complicates definitions focusing on modeling languages.

A usability study would be of limited value if it would not be based on a standard definition and operationalization of usability [Coursaris and Kim, 2006].

The International Organization for Standardization (ISO) defines usability as the capacity of the software product to be understood, learned and attractive to the user, when it is used under specified conditions [ISO/IEC9241-110, 2006].

Additionally, the ISO defined another standard which describes usability as the extent to which a product can be used by specified users to achieve specified goals with effectiveness, efficiency and satisfaction in a specified context of use [ISO/IEC9241-11, 1998].

The Institute of Electrical and Electronics Engineers (IEEE) established a standard, which describes usability as the ease a user can learn how to operate, prepare inputs for, understand and interpret the outputs of a system or component [IEEE610.12-1990, 1990].

Dumas and Redish (1999) define, usability means quickness and simplicity regarding a user's task accomplishment. This definition is based on four assumptions [Dumas and Redish, 1999]:

1. Usability means focusing on users,

2. Usability includes productivity,

3. Usability means ease of use,

4. Usability means efficient task accomplishment.

Shackel (1991) associates five attributes for defining usability [Shackel, 1991]:

- Speed

- Time to learn

- Retention

- Errors

- User specific attitude

Preece et al. (1994) combined effectiveness and efficiency to throughput [Preece et al., 1994]. Constantine and Lockwood (1999) and Nielsen (2006) collected the attributes defining usability and developed an overall definition of usability attributes consisting of learnability, memorability, effectiveness, efficiency and user satisfaction [Constantine and Lockwood, 1999, Nielsen, 2006a].

The variety of definitions concerning usability attributes led to the use of different terms and labels for the same usability characteristics, or different terms for similar characteristics, without full consistency across these standards; in general, the situation in the literature is similar. For example, learnability is defined in ISO 9241-11 as a simple attribute, "time of learning", whereas ISO 9126 defines it as including several attributes such as "comprehensible input and output, instructions readiness, messages readiness ..." [ISO/IEC9241-11, 1998, Abran et al., 2003, ISO/IEC9126-1:2001, 2004].

4.2.2. Defining User Scenarios

When considering the user of modeling languages regarding a usability evaluation, each user can be exposed to different situations. Some may be primarily involved with the development of models, while others may be primarily involved with interpretation of models [Siau and Wang, 2007].

Thus, different requirements depending on the specific situation can be defined. A model developer (e.g. a software engineer) needs:

- to learn a modeling language within a short period of time,

- to remember the language's elements and syntax to ensure correct models,

- to reach a fast and correct task accomplishment,

- to be satisfied with the modeling language.

A model interpreter needs to recognize both the process flow and the structure of a model. Due to this fact, a model interpreter requires an intuitive and explicit model regarding shapes, model structure and syntax. For evaluating the usability of modeling languages it is essential to differentiate between these two situations [Schalles et al., 2010a].

However, on a user level the boundaries between these two different scenarios may be blurred. For example, a software developer reads a model for supporting the code development of an application system. The same software developer may create models of existing apllication systems for analyzing possible system weaknesses [Figl et al., 2010]. In the FUEML framework this effect is not considered and consequently, the two different user scenarios are strictly separated throughout the empirical results and the findings of this thesis.

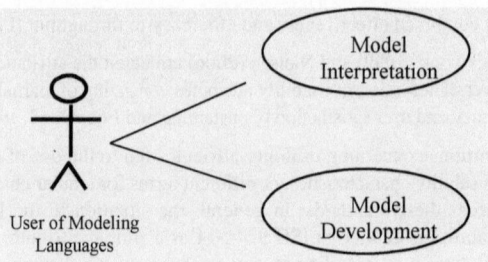

Figure 4.2.1.: Use Cases in the Modeling Domain

4.2.3. Extracting appropriate Usability Attributes for Modeling Languages

Considering the different usability definitions it is possible to extract attributes for developing a usability definition focusing on modeling languages. This evaluation framework proposes to use the five usability attributes of

- *Learnability,*
- *Memorability,*
- *Effectiveness,*
- *Efficiency and*
- *User Satisfaction* specified by [Constantine and Lockwood, 1999, Nielsen, 1993].

Research has shown that the role of the user's visual attention can provide additional information on usability testing [Sibert and Jacob, 2000].

In usability engineering eye-tracking assists software designers to evaluate the usability of screen layouts. The evaluation of the user's visual attention cannot be measured by traditional usability attributes [Pretorius et al., 2005].

Integrating eye-tracking into FUEML provides additional knowledge that is not obtained from traditional usability testing methods [Karn et al., 1999].

Therefore, I introduced the

- *Perceptibility*

as a sixth usability attribute.

In the following, each attribute is defined regarding the usability evaluation of modeling languages:

Learnability is probably the most important attribute of usability, since a modeling language needs to be easy to learn. Learning to use a modeling language seems to be the first experience most users are confronted with a new modeling language [Siau and Rossi, 2008, Mayer, 1989].

Memorability describes the "remembering rate" of a modeling language. Overall it describes the fact that a modeling language should be easy to remember regarding its elements, syntax and semantics [Recker and Dreiling, 2007, Mayer, 1989].

Effectiveness characterises the fact, that it should be possible to reach a successful task accomplishment. In this regard, a user should be able to develop and comprehend models with low error rates [Bobkowska, 2005b, Wand and Weber, 1993].

Efficiency refers to users with medium-high modeling experience. Once a user has learned a modeling language it should be possible to reach a high level of productivity. A modeling language is efficient to use when the users are able to develop or comprehend a model relatively quickly and correctly regarding the regulations of the modeling language [Wand and Weber, 1993, Bobkowska, 2005a].

User Satisfaction focuses on the user and his/her subjective contentment when modeling or interpreting a model [Siau and Wang, 2007].

Perceptibility is a very important attribute for evaluating the usability of modeling languages. In most instances this attribute relates to the interpretation of models. This attribute is measured by using the method of eye-tracking, which can be described as a technique to determine eye movement and eye fixation patterns of a user [Moody and Heymans, 2010]. Regarding this evaluation framework, the additional information by using this technique can answer questions such as does the user recognize the process flow or the diagram structure of the model in an easy way?

A general definition of usability indicating how it is applied to modeling languages in this thesis is presented as follows:

> *The usability of modeling languages is specified by learnability, memorability, effectiveness, efficiency, user satisfaction and perceptibility. The learnability of modeling languages describes the capability of a modeling language to enable the user to learn how to use it. The modeling language and its semantics, syntax and elements should be easy to remember, so that a user is able to return to the language after some period of non-use without having to learn the language again. The modeling language should be effective for reaching a successful task accomplishment. The modeling language should be efficient to use, so that a high level of working productivity is possible. The modeling language should be pleasant to use. Users have to be satisfied when using the language. The language should offer a convenient perceptibility regarding structure, overview, elements and shapes.*

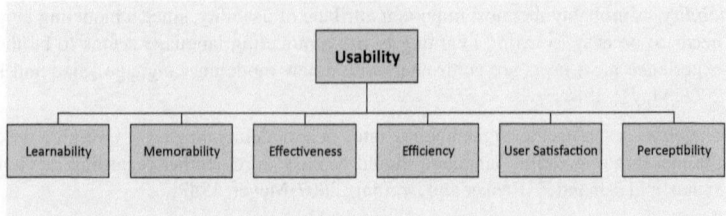

Figure 4.2.2.: Usability Attributes in the Domain of graphical Modeling Languages

4.3. Developing Usability Metrics

For measuring usability it is important to define metrics depending on the restrictive investigation object [Seffah et al., 2006].

Before developing usability metrics, it is useful to introduce a formal definition of graphical modeling languages. For the following definition predicate logical terms are used.

Graphical modeling languages aim to support the development of graphs. Let $y(x)$ be the number of node-elements and $z(x)$ the number of edge-elements and $x \in M$ with $M = ModelingLanguage$ it is concluded that a modeling language consist of nodes and edges. All graphical modeling languages contain nodes and edges as mandatory parts of a modeling language.

If n is a node and e an edge such that

$$\psi G(e) = \{n, n'\}$$

then e is said to join n and n', and the nodes n and n' are called the ends of e. As a consequence we have

$$n = \{n_1 ... n_n\} \text{ and } e = \{n_1 x n_n\} \text{ with } \{n_1, n_n\} \in M.$$

No graph and consequently no graphical modeling language can exist without nodes and edges [Diestel, 2005].

Concerning the usability of modeling languages some metrics are basically functions that are defined in terms of a formula but others are simple countable data. In the following, usability metrics for modeling languages are developed and assigned to the attributes defined in the previous section.

In order to assess the usability of modeling languages an additional possibility is to use the method of eye-tracking [Gordon, 2004, Das et al., 2008, Ehmke and Wilson, 2007, Pretorius et al., 2005].

4.3.1. Effectiveness

Evaluating Effectiveness F requires the analysis of a task output with measuring quantity and quality of goal achievement [Rengger et al., 1993].

Quantity is defined as the proportion of task goals represented in the output of a task. Quality is the degree to which the task goals represented in the output have been achieved [Bevan and Macleod, 1994].

Bevan (1995) defined Effectiveness as a product of Quantity and Quality [Bevan, 1995].

Transferring this issue to FUEML, effectiveness can be expressed in the following formula with applying the number of nodes N, edges E and errors R of a model developed or interpreted as metrics for proband's task completion and task goals [Kan, 2002]:

$$Effectiveness\,(F) = Grade\,of\,completeness * Grade\,of\,correctness \qquad (4.3.1)$$

$$Grade\,of\,completeness = \frac{\sum (N_{task} + E_{task})}{\sum (N_{goals} + E_{goals})}, D = \{0; 1\} \qquad (4.3.2)$$

$$Grade\,of\,correctness = \frac{\sum (N_{goals} + E_{goals} - R)}{\sum (N_{goals} + E_{goals})}, D = \{0; 1\} \qquad (4.3.3)$$

A limitation of this metric exists when the nodes and edges of a task model are greater than the nodes and edges of the goal model. Consequently the domain of this metric is restricted to values between zero and one.

4.3.2. Efficiency

The Efficiency G is the amount of human, economical and temporal resources. Measures of efficiency relate to the level of effectiveness achieved to the expenditure of resources [Bevan and Macleod, 1994].

Measure values of efficiency include time taken to complete tasks [Vuolle et al., 2008].

Hence, this can be expressed by the ratio of Effectiveness F and Task Completion Time T in minutes:

$$Efficiency(G) = \frac{F}{T} \tag{4.3.4}$$

4.3.3. Learnability

Learnability describes the ease of learning the semantics and syntax including different shapes and the application of these elements. For this characteristic, the standard measure values are based on time behavior (task completion time, interpretation time) and the accuracy [Seffah et al., 2006].

In general, learnability is a development and can be graphically described by learning curves [Tamir et al., 2008].

Hence, learnability can be measured by the rate of difference when the user repeats evaluation sessions [Bevan, 1995].

Nielsen (1993) insists that highly learnable systems could be categorized as "allowing users to reach a reasonable level of usage proficiency within a short time" [Nielsen, 1993].

Furthermore, Nielsen (2006) proposes measuring proficiency by quantity, quality and time behavior of goal achievement. Thus, the defined efficiency metric is equal to proficiency and can be applied for measuring learnability [Nembhard and Napassavong, 2002, Grossman et al., 2009].

With conducting two measuring points mp and $mp + 1$, it is possible to analyze the relative difference between mp and $mp + 1$ based on efficiency (G) for indicating Δ Learnability in percent :

$$\Delta Learnability = \frac{G_{mp+1} - G_{mp}}{G_{mp}} \tag{4.3.5}$$

In the following, the presented metrics are demonstrated and proved by an example. Participants are asked to develop a process model based on a given textual process description. The example models are presented in Figure 4.3.1.

The goal model with $N = 4 \wedge E = 3$ is the model requested and the task model with $N = 2 \wedge E = 1$ is the possible output of one participant.

The task model contains one error due to the fact that an EPC-model must start with a triggering event (purple). Furthermore, it is presumed that the task model was generated in *120 seconds* by participant.

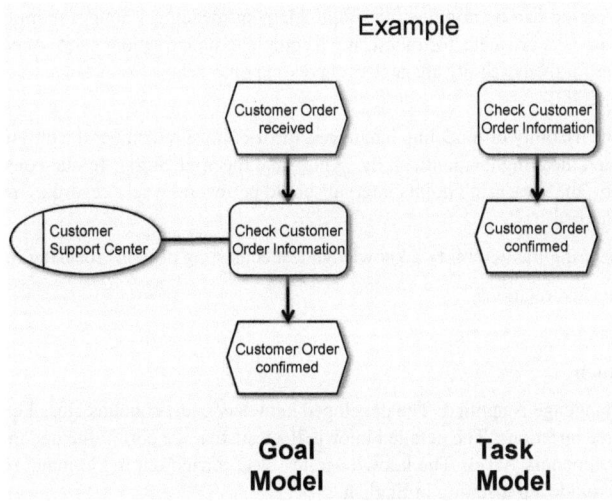

Figure 4.3.1.: Example Models for demonstrating the Usability Metrics

Based on this, the calculation of the developed metrics for effectiveness, efficiency and learnability is shown:

$$Effectiveness\,(F) = \frac{2+1}{4+3} * \frac{4+3-1}{4+3} = 0.43 * 0.86 = 0.37$$

$$Efficiency = \frac{0.37}{2m} = 0.19$$

Considering that a 0.19 is the value for efficiency in session 1 and a possible value for session 2 is 0.30 leads to the following calculation of learnability:

$$Learnability = \frac{0.30 - 0.19}{0.19} = 0.58$$

The given examples show that the metrics result in values that are comparable between different modeling languages in a survey.

4.3.4. Memorability

Memorability is best measured as proficiency after a period of non-use provided a user has already learned a language [Olle et al., 1986].

The non-use period can be minutes for simple element meanings, hours for simple syntactic regulations and days or weeks for measuring a complete modeling language. Accordingly, the measure values for memorability are neglect curves and time-delayed knowledge tests [Nembhard and Uzumeri, 2000].

Concerning the usability of modeling languages, the user must remember the different elements and its intended meaning (semantics), the syntax and the application. In due consideration of Nielsen (2006), the measuring points interval should be several weeks regarding memorability [Nielsen, 2006a].

Thus, for measuring memorability a knowledge test consisting of items focusing on

- elements and relations,

- syntax and

- application

of particular language is applied. The developed knowledge test contains closed questions and multiple-choice questions. The detailed knowledge tests that are part of the upcoming surveys are shown in appendix A.1.3. The knowledge test was carried out in German. However, the impressions provide a translation in English.

Knowledge Test

1.) Age: _____

2.) Gender: ☐ male   ☐ female

3.) Your knowledge of the English language is

☐ native   ☐ fluent   ☐ beginner

4.) How many models did you develop or interpret approximately?

☐ none

☐ < 10

☐ > 10

5.) How many UML Class Diagrams did you develop or interpret approximately?

☐ none

☐ < 10

☐ > 10

6.) Please name all elements of UML Class Diagrams you can remember spontaneously!

_____

_____

_____

7.) Please name all possible relations between the elements of UML Class Diagrams you can remember spontaneously!

_____

_____

_____

_____

8.)   Evaluate the following statements by ticking one box per phrase

	Correct	Wrong	
A class consist of a name, attributes and operations	☐	☐	(4.1)
The Generalization relationship indicates the subclass is considered to be a specialized form of the super type and a superclass is considered as ' Generalization of a subclass	☐	☐	(4.2)
Associations describe the relationship between a composite and its parts	☐	☐	(4.3)
Generalizations can be specified through adding cardinalities	☐	☐	(4.4)
Abstract classes may not be instantiated and require subclasses to provide implementations for the abstract methods	☐	☐	(4.5)
Multiplicities describe the number of objects that participate in a relationship between classes	☐	☐	(4.6)
A composition is a directed edge	☐	☐	(4.7)

9.) Please cross out incorrect models!

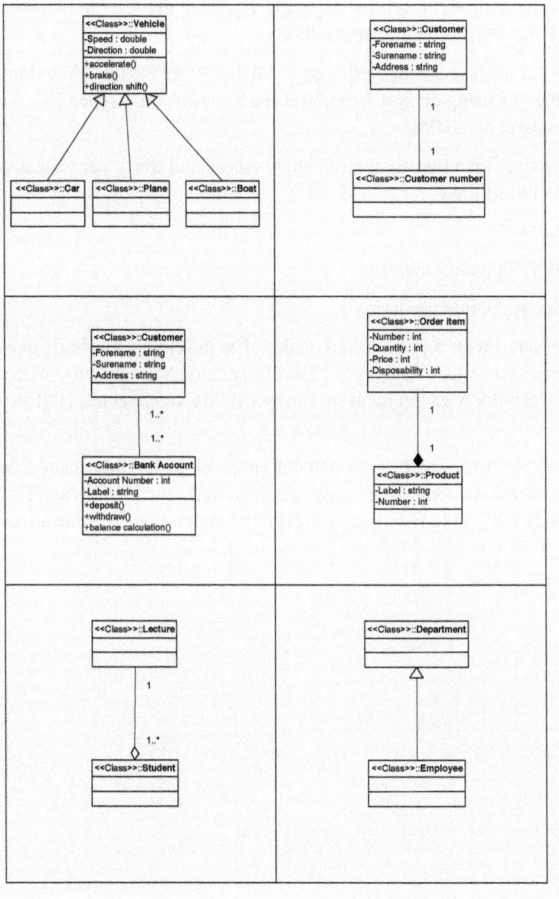

4.3.5. User Satisfaction

Compared to the other latent variables in this thesis, the individual satisfaction of a user while developing or interpreting a model is a user subjective criterion that can be measured best by using standardized questionnaires [Vuolle et al., 2008].

Currently no standardized method for measuring user satisfaction in the modeling domain exists. Therefore, questionnaires focusing on system and website usability are mapped [Kirakowski and Corbett, 1993, Armstrong et al., 2005].

For evaluating user satisfaction a questionnaire, which consists of thirty items, was developed. The items are structured as follows:

- General impression
- Satisfaction in development scenarios
- Satisfaction in interpretation scenarios

The constructs are measured with 5-point Likert-scales. The development of this questionnaire is generally contributing to the Questionnaire for User Interaction Satisfaction (QUIS) and additionally the Software Usability Measurement Inventory (SUMI) [Chin et al., 1988, Kirakowski and Corbett, 1993].

In addition to that, variables focusing on user perception developed by Maes and Poels (2007) for measuring user satisfaction in our model were specified and added [Maes and Poels, 2007]. The questionnaire was carried out in German. However, the impressions provide a translation in English.

Questionnaire

1.) Age: _____

2.) Gender: ☐ male   ☐ female

3.) Your knowledge of the English language is
     ☐ native   ☐ fluent   ☐ beginner

4.) How many models did you develop or interpret approximately?
     ☐ none
     ☐ < 10
     ☐ > 10

5.) How many <<language the survey is focused on>> did you develop or interpret approximately?
     ☐ none
     ☐ < 10
     ☐ > 10

6.) Please rate if you disagree or agree with the following statements

General Impressions	strongly disagree	disagree	uncertain	agree	strongly agree
I am likely to choose this language for modeling/interpreting my business cases	☐	☐	☐	☐	☐
I recommend this language without any concerns	☐	☐	☐	☐	☐
The application of this language is circumstantial	☐	☐	☐	☐	☐
The application of this language is frustrating	☐	☐	☐	☐	☐
My expectations for that language are fulfilled	☐	☐	☐	☐	☐

Model Development	strongly disagree	disagree	uncertain	agree	strongly agree
Developing a model by applying this language was easy	☐	☐	☐	☐	☐
Developing a model by applying this language was successful	☐	☐	☐	☐	☐
I was able to develop the given scenario completely	☐	☐	☐	☐	☐
I was able to develop the given scenario accurately	☐	☐	☐	☐	☐
The number of different elements and relations in language's metamodel are confusing	☐	☐	☐	☐	☐
The syntax of the modeling language is confusing	☐	☐	☐	☐	☐
It was difficult to remember language's elements	☐	☐	☐	☐	☐
Remembering language's syntax was difficult	☐	☐	☐	☐	☐
I am likely to choose the language for modeling business cases	☐	☐	☐	☐	☐

Model Interpretation	strongly disagree	disagree	uncertain	agree	strongly agree
Interpretation of given model was easy	☐	☐	☐	☐	☐
Comprehending the meaning of given model was successful	☐	☐	☐	☐	☐
Comprehending the meaning of given model was complete	☐	☐	☐	☐	☐
Comprehending the meaning of given model was fast	☐	☐	☐	☐	☐
Remembering different elements during model interpretation was difficult	☐	☐	☐	☐	☐
Remembering language's syntax during model interpretation was difficult	☐	☐	☐	☐	☐
I am likely to choose the language for interpreting business cases	☐	☐	☐	☐	☐

7. **Please mark your overall satisfaction with the modelling language on the following line!**

Totally unsatisfied ———————————————————————— Very satisfied

4.3.6. Visual Perceptibility

The visual perceptibility focusing on model interpretation scenarios is measured by using the method of eye tracking with analyzing the user's visual attention [Gordon, 2004].

In this research eye tracking is included for measuring user's cognitive processes i.e. information search and information extraction during a model interpretation process.

The pioneering work regarding the use of eye tracking was first carried out by Fitts et al. (1950) [Fitts et al., 1950]. They proposed that fixation length is a measure of difficulty of information extraction and interpretation.

Fixations are eye movements that stabilize the gaze over an object of interest. During this, the brain starts to process the visual information received from the eyes [Duchowski, 2007].

The number of fixations overall is an indicator for the search efficiency in an eye-tracking experiment [Goldberg and Kotval, 1999].

Consequently, a larger number of fixations indicates less efficient search in a model. Concerning an eye tracking experiment for evaluating the visual perceptibility of modeling languages a large number of fixations implies an intensive search to explore the model's diagram structure. This fact complicates the interpretation of a model.

A further objective is the analysis of difficulty of information extraction in a model. Byrne et al. (1999) propose the tracking of *fixation duration* time as a measure for information extraction [Byrne et al., 1999] .

From this follows that longer fixation times during an interpretation process are indicating a participant's difficulty extracting information from a model.

4.3.7. Prior Knowledge

Intuitively, it is assumed that human's current behavior in the modeling domain is influenced by prior knowledge in model development and model interpretation. For example, users with plenty prior knowledge in modeling would conduct development and interpretation tasks faster and more correct compared to less experienced users. First, there is a need to define prior knowledge in the modeling domain. Prior knowledge of a domain result in "(...) an understanding of its basic contents, as well as its goals, rules and/or principles (...)" [Chiese et al., 1979]. Transferring this in the area of modeling languages, prior modeling knowledge result in a general understanding of basic semantic and syntactic language concepts and, consequently, the correct application of the language in development and interpretation scenarios [Schalles et al., 2010a].

For measuring participant's prior modeling knowledge in an empirical survey, the experience in modeling and particular languages has to be recorded. In conjunction with the research described in this thesis, survey participant's model experience is collected by tracking individual experience in

1. general modeling experience and
2. language experience

on a 3-point Likert-scale separated by interpretation and development scenarios.

> **How many models did you develop or interpret approximately?**
>
> □ none
>
> □ < 10
>
> □ > 10

> **How many UML Class Diagrams did you develop or interpret approximately?**
>
> □ none
>
> □ < 10
>
> □ > 10

4.4. Defining usability-influencing Metaproperties of Modeling Languages

In the following section a determination of language-based properties influencing the usability of graphical modeling languages is conducted. For evaluating the usability of modeling languages it is additionally essential to operationalize the language semantics and syntax properties. Modeling languages are based on metamodels defining the language's semantics and syntax [Karagiannis and Kühn, 2002].

The syntax subsumes all regulations concerning the formal structure of a modeling language including the syntactic notation, which can be described as a set of elements [Havey, 2005]. The different elements of modeling languages feature an heterogeneous appearance regarding shapes and colors. The semantics describe the element's intended meaning within the modeling language.

As a consequence, the metaproperties of modeling languages have a visual and a complexity-related character. In the following chapters, those two different forms of metaproperties of modeling languages are introduced and operationalized.

4.4.1. Visual Properties

Graphical languages differ from textual languages such as programming languages in how they encode information and how they are processed by the human mind.

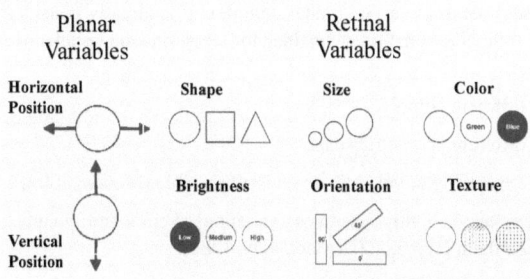

Figure 4.4.1.: Design Properties of Language Elements

Textual languages encode information using sequences of characters, while visual languages encode information using spatial arrangements of graphic and textual elements. Textual representations are 1-dimensional, whereas visual representations are 2-dimensional: A widely accepted definition of a diagram is a representation in which information is indexed by 2-dimensional location [Larkin and Simon, 1987].

According to dual channel theory, the human mind has separate systems for processing pictorial and verbal material [Mayer and Moreno, 2003].

Visual representations are processed in parallel by the visual system, while textual representations are processed serially by the auditory system [Bertin, 1983].

These differences mean that fundamentally different principles are required for evaluating and designing visual languages. However, such principles are far less developed than those available for textual languages [Gurr, 1999, Winn, 1990].

Moody (2010) deduces visual variables from Bertin's Semiology of Graphics that need to be optimized for processing by the human mind [Bertin, 1983].

Bertin (1983) identified eight visual variables that can be used to graphically encode information. These are divided into planar variables (the two spatial dimensions) and retinal variables (features of the retinal image). Planar variables are position-based and subsume the horizontal and vertical position of diagram components while retinal variables describe element-based properties such as shape, size, color, brightness, orientation and texture [Moody and Heymans, 2010].

Structuring those variables leads to variables with color properties (color, brightness, texture) and one variable with geometric properties (shape), which are defined in the metamodel of a graphical modeling language.

Contrariwise, the planar variables and additionally size and orientation depend on the particular model developed or interpreted.

However, the model perspective i.e. model complexity is already considered in this survey. Consequently, the following variables are defined for measuring the visual dimension of graphical modeling languages:

- Number of different colors

- Number of different geometric shapes

Color is one of the most cognitively effective visual variable [Moody, 2009].

The human visual system is highly sensitive to variations in color and can quickly and accurately distinguish between them [Winn, 2002, Mackinlay, 1986].

Differences in color are detected three times faster than shape and are also more easily remembered [Treisman, 1982, Lohse, 1993].

However, color is rarely used in SE notations and is specifically prohibited in UML 2.0:

> "UML avoids the use of graphic markers, such as color, that present challenges for certain persons (the color blind) and for important kinds of equipment (such as printers, copiers, and fax machines)" [OMG, 2005b] .

However, color should never be used as the sole basis for distinguishing between symbols as it is sensitive to variations in visual perception (e.g., color blindness) and screen/printer characteristics (e.g., black-and-white printers).

To avoid loss of information (robust design), color should only be used for redundant coding. Event-driven Process Chains (EPCs) is one of few graphical modeling languages using color to encode information. But this language makes the mistake of using it in a non-redundant way.

When diagrams are reproduced in black and white, differences between some symbols disappear [Moody, 2009].

4.4.2. Language Complexity

The quality of a complexity measure rests on its explanatory power and applicability. Explanatory power refers to the measure's ability to explain the interrelationships among complexity, quality, and other programming and design parameters. Applicability refers to the degree to which the measure can be applied to improve the quality of work during the design, coding and testing stages [Siau and Cao, 2001].

For measuring the complexity of graphical modeling languages Welke (1992) and additionally Rossi and Brinkkemper (1996) developed several metrics generally based on the OPRR (Object, Property, Relationship, Role) data model [Welke, 1992, Rossi and Brinkkemper, 1996].

The metrics in their essence are based on calculations of the counts of object types O, relationship types R and property types P of a method. These fundamental counts allow the derivation of the

Language	O	R	P	$C(M)$
EPC	15	5	11	19.26
BPMN	90	6	143	169.07
UML Class Diagrams	7	18	18	26.40
UML Activity Diagrams	8	5	6	11.18
UML Use Case Diagram	6	6	6	10.39
UML Component Diagram	8	10	9	15.65

Table 4.1.: Complexity Values for heterogeneous Modeling Languages [Recker et al., 2009, Indulska et al., 2009]

average number of properties per object type, average number of properties per relationship type, and the average number of relationship types that can be linked with a particular object type in a given method. All of which indicate the complexity of of describing relationship types or object types in a given method. These metrics form the basis for the calculation of the total conceptual complexity of a method, which can then be used as a benchmark for comparison of conceptual complexity of different methods [Rossi and Brinkkemper, 1996].

$$C(M) = \sqrt{O^2 + R^2 + P^2} \qquad (4.4.1)$$

Several researchers such as Indulska et al. (2009) and Recker et al. (2009) transferred those metrics to UML diagrams, EPC's and the BPMN [Indulska et al., 2009, Recker et al., 2009]. Table 4.1 shows a brief comparison concerning the complexity $C(M)$ of heterogenous modeling languages.

4.5. The FUEML Framework

In the previous chapters the components of the developed FUEML Framework were deduced theoretically. Furthermore, the different attributes measuring usability were extracted and metrics were developed.

The next step is the subsumption of these components in one evaluation framework. As shown in the previous chapters the framework requires several components that are important of an evaluation framework in the domain of graphical modeling languages.

These components are:

- Consideration of *Model Development and Model Interpretation Scenarios*
- Consideration of *Language Properties*, which are influencing the usability of graphical modeling languages
- Consideration of different *Usability Attributes* and *Metrics*

Figure 4.5.1 shows the FUEML Framework in a causal diagram picturing the interaction of the extracted components for measuring the usability of graphical modeling languages. Additional causal interactions between the different usability attributes are deduced and developed in chapter 8 of this thesis.

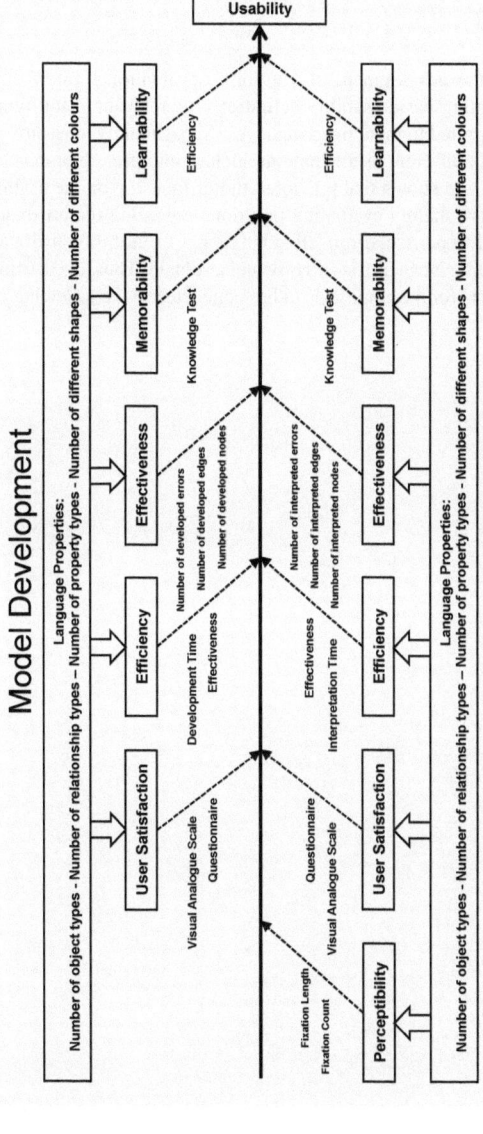

Figure 4.5.1.: The FUEML Framework

4.6. Conclusion

This chapter presented the development of a usability evaluation framework for modeling languages. After elaborating basic usability definitions the relevant usability attributes were extracted, adopted and applied to modeling languages. Subsequently, measure values for each attribute were defined and different user situations such as interpreting or developing a model have been considered. It was shown that previous studies focusing on the usability evaluation of modeling languages are mainly evaluating partitions regarding the attributes of usability. These studies are limited to particular modeling languages or usability attributes. An overall usability survey for modeling languages is currently not available. Thus, the developed evaluation framework provides a basis for the empirical studies conducted in the following chapters of this thesis.

5. Developing a Generic Metric For Measuring Model Complexity

In recent years, various object and process oriented modeling methods were developed to support the process of modeling in enterprises. When applying these methods, graphical models are generated and used to depict various aspects of enterprise architectures. Concerning this, surveys analyzing modeling languages in different ways were conducted. In many cases these surveys include experimental data collection methods. At this juncture the complexity of concrete models often affects output of these studies. To ensure complexity value comparability of different models, a generic metric for measuring complexity of models is proposed. Another variable impacting on the output of a usability study in the domain of graphical modeling languages is the complexity of different tasks applied. Since we move in the area of modeling languages, a metric measuring task complexity by defining complexity of models that have to be developed or interpreted by survey participants is developed. This ensures comparability of survey results crossing different modeling languages. In this chapter the development of a generic metric measuring model complexity (GCMM) is proposed. The developed metric is evaluated and applied in the empirical surveys in this thesis [Schalles et al., 2010c].

Even though software and process modeling have been used intensely over the last decades, only a small number of research analyzed understandability and comprehension of graphical models [Mendling and Strembeck, 2008].

Past researches either were focusing on process models or structural models. For example, Mendling (2008) developed metrics for process models such as Event Driven Process Chains (EPC) [Mendling, 2008].

Metrics in software engineering have shown their potential as guidance to improve software designs and make them more understandable and easier to maintain [Vanderfeesten et al., 2007a].

Surveys focusing on the evaluation of modeling languages include metrics measuring model complexity in order to operationalize the influence of model complexity on particular outputs. When analyzing these studies it appears that a great number of empirical researches apply easy structured metrics for measuring the complexity of models. This chapter focuses on the development of a generic metric for measuring the complexity of process models e.g. EPC as well as structure models and UML Class Diagrams. Several researchers concluded that business process and software program designs have a lot in common [Vanderfeesten et al., 2007b, Reijers and Vanderfeesten, 2005]. In general, this metric aims at researchers conducting empirical surveys on modeling languages.

The quality of a complexity measure rests on its explanatory power and applicability. Explanatory power refers to the measure's ability to explain the interrelationships among complexity, quality, and other programming and design parameters. Applicability refers to the degree to which the measure can be applied to improve the quality of work during the design, coding and testing stages [Siau and Cao, 2001].

5.1. Overview of related Complexity Measures in Literature

There are several major complexity measures in the literature, which are analyzed in the following section.

5.1.1. Lines of Code

Lines of code is a count of instruction statements. Because the lines of code count represents the program size and complexity, it is not a surprise that the more lines of code there are in a program, the more defects should be expected. A concave relationship between number of defects and module size was suggested. Withrow (1990) examined modules written in Ada for a large project at Unisys and confirmed the concave relationship between defect density and module size [Withrow, 1990].

The author argued that there might be an optimal program size that could lead to the lowest defect rate. As module size becomes large, the complexity increases to a level beyond a programmer's immediate span of control and total comprehension.

However, for calculating model complexity this metric seems to be not suitable because it is focused on coding software and not models.

5.1.2. Halstead's Software Science

Halstead (1977) developed a system of equations expressing the total vocabulary, overall program length, potential minimum volume for an algorithm, program level (a measure of software complexity), program difficulty, and other features such as development effort and projected number of faults in the software. Halstead metrics are static metrics, ignoring the huge variations in fault rates observed in software products and among modules [Halstead, 1977].

5.1.3. Cyclomatic Complexity

The cyclomatic complexity measure by McCabe (1976) is designed to indicate a program's testability and understandability. The measure provides the classical graph theory cyclomatic number, indicating the number of regions in a graph. The cyclomatic complexity metric is additive. The complexity of several graphs that form a group is equal to the sum of the individual graph's complexities [Mc Cabe, 1976].

5.1.4. Structure Metrics

Lines of code, Halstead's software science, and McCabe's cyclomatic complexity metrics that measure module complexity assume implicitly that each program module is a separate entity [Kan, 2002].

Structure metrics try to take into account the interactions between modules in a product or system and quantify such interactions. Weyuker (1988) examined and compared four complexity measures – Lines of code, Halstead's software science, McCabe's cyclomatic complexity metrics, and structure metrics. She discussed the proper use of structure metrics in object-oriented software evaluation and called for a more rigorous study on complexity measures, which would lead to the definition of good meaningful software complexity measures [Weyuker, 1988].

Many approaches in structure metrics have been proposed. Some examples include system-partitioning measures by Belady and Evangelisti (1981), information flow metrics by Henry and Kafura (1981), and stability measures by Yau and Collofello (1980) [Belady and Evangelisti, 1981, Henry and Kafura, 1981, Yau and Collofello, 1985].

More recently, Rossi & Brinkkemper (1994) introduced seventeen complexity metrics for systems development methods and techniques [Rossi and Brinkkemper, 1996].

5.2. Size

For developing a generic model complexity metric analogous partitions of complexity metrics are transformed. Halstead (1977) and Mc Cabe (1976) propose a set of metrics including primitive measure values for measuring software complexity [Halstead, 1977, Mc Cabe, 1976].

Firstly, in this approach it is suggested to map model elements and relations to a set of primitive measures proposed by Halstead (1977) and Mc Cabe (1976). For example, the number of unique operator occurences and the number of operand occurrences are the number of nodes N and edges E in a model. With the size S is dependent on E and R the following formula can be defined:

$$S = \sum (N + E) \qquad (5.2.1)$$

5.3. Semantic Spread

Models developed in different domains and with different methods differ very often not only syntactically but also semantically [Pfeiffer, 2007].

With focusing on the development of a generic complexity metric, the particular semantic complexity differences between models have to be considered. Esswein et al. (2004) differentiate between semantics of modeling language constructs *(abstract semantics)* and semantics of each model statement *(concrete semantics)* [Esswein et al., 2004].

To ensure the generic aim, GCMM focuses on abstract semantics (i.e. Event, Function, Activity, Class etc.). For measuring the semantic spread L of a concrete model, the number of semantic different nodes N_{dif} and the number of semantic different edges E_{dif} are introduced. Recker and Dreiling (2007) propose these concepts for measuring model complexity [Recker and Dreiling, 2007].

From this, the following definition of L is deduced:

$$L = \sum \left(N_{dif} + E_{dif} \right) \qquad (5.3.1)$$

5.4. Connectivity

Beside size and semantic spread a further important part of the metric is density. One essential element for measuring model density is described by connectivity degree of contained arcs and vertices [Mendling, 2008].

In general, the developed connectivity degree metric is based on Yang et al. (2006) [Yang et al., 2006]. For measuring the connectivity degree of ontologies they propose the ratio of relations and arcs. With adding Henry and Kafura's approach to the metric, the complexity of element's connections to its environment is captured [Henry and Kafura, 1981].

Hence, the *fan-in* and *fan-out* metric maps to number of element inputs N_{In} and number of element outputs N_{Out} in a particular model. Finally, the described concepts result in the following formula for measuring the connectivity degree c of various models:

$$c = \frac{\sum (N_{In} + N_{Out})}{\sum N} = \frac{\sum E * 2}{\sum N} \tag{5.4.1}$$

Considering Ince and Hekmatpur (1988) the term $\sum (N_{In} + N_{Out})$ can be simplified by $\sum E * 2$ [Ince and Hekmatpur, 1988].

5.5. Generic Complexity Metric

In due consideration of different analyzed and developed metric properties we are able to build up our generic model complexity metric. Table 5.1 summarizes the above and gives an overview of different metric properties and their source of derivation.

The developed metric contains size S, semantic spread L and connectivity degree c for measuring the complexity of models. In general, a linear relation between C_M and $S; L$ is proposed. Considering the fact that semantic spread increases user related complexity more than model size the squaring of L is introduced.

Hence, L^2 weights semantic spread more than S of particular model. For example, the more different relationships (e.g. generalization, aggregation etc) are used in a class diagram the higher seems complexity of this model. Root extraction over $S + L^2$ lowers value dispersion to a significant level. Furthermore this result is weighted with model connectivity degree.

Thus, the following formula for generic measurement of model complexity C_M is proposed:

$$C_M = \sqrt{(S + L^2)} * c \tag{5.5.1}$$

Derivation	Extracted Components
Mc Cabe (1976), Halstead (1977)	Number of nodes N
Mc Cabe (1976), Halstead (1977)	Number of edges E
Henry and Kafura (1981)	Number of node inputs N_{in}
Henry and Kafura (1981)	Number of node outputs N_{out}
Recker and Dreiling (2007)	Semantic different nodes N_{dif}
Recker and Dreiling (2007)	Semantic different edges E_{dif}
Yang et al. (2006)	Connectivity degree c

Table 5.1.: Overview of different Model Complexity Metric Properties

Model	S	L	c	C_M
Class Diagram I	11	3	1.67	7.45
EPC I	9	4	1.60	8.00
Activity Diagram I	14	5	2.00	12.49
Class Diagram II	25	7	1.92	16.49
EPC II	45	5	2.09	17.49
EPC III	63	8	1.90	21.45

Table 5.2.: Complexity Calculation with GCMM

5.6. Evaluation of the developed Complexity Metric

In order to prove correctness and reliability of the developed metric, the complexity of six heterogeneous models is calculated applying GCMM. Therefore, models with different complexity degrees are chosen. For proving the generality of GCMM, different structure and process modeling languages are applied. Figure 5.6.1 gives an overview of the applied models.

Additionally, Table 5.2 shows resulting variables S, L, and c with applying the developed complexity metric GCMM.

For testing the correlation between metric results and individual complexity evaluation we conducted a survey on complexity of models. In this experiment overall 20 modeling experts participated. They were asked to evaluate the complexity of models pictured in Figure 5.6.1 on a scale with extreme values 1 and 10.

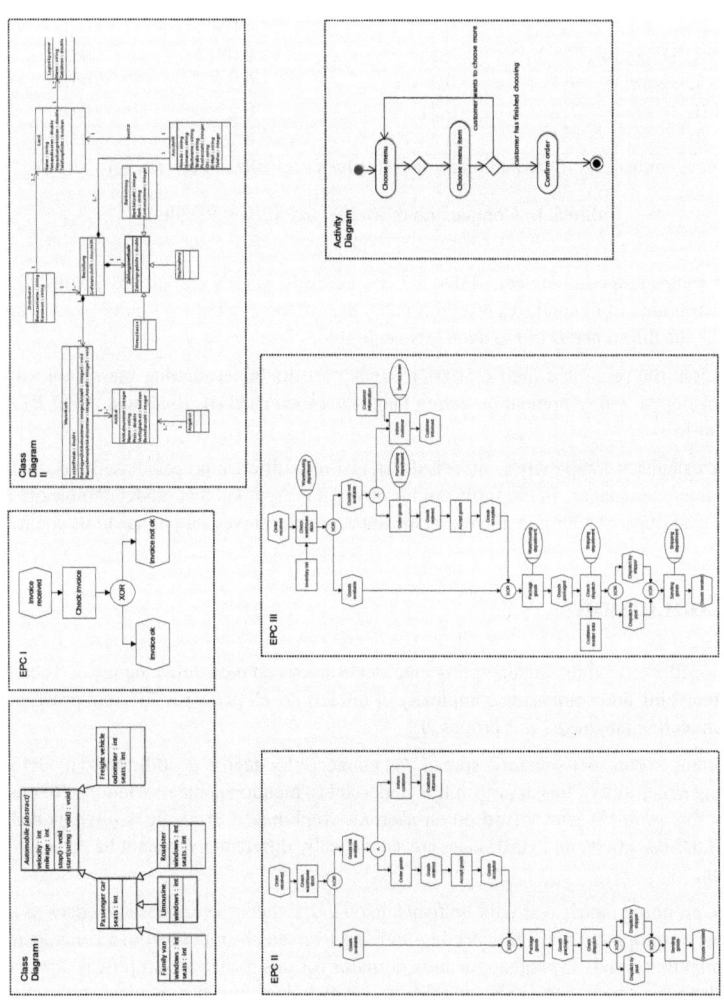

Figure 5.6.1.: Heterogeneous Models evaluated with GCMM

Model	C_S	rel. Distribution C_M*	rel. Distribution C_S*	D
Class Diagram I	2.3	0.09	0.08	0.01
EPC I	1.5	0.10	0.05	0.05
Activity Diagram	2.8	0.15	0.09	0.06
Class Diagram II	7.3	0.20	0.24	0.04
EPC II	7.7	0.21	0.25	0.04
EPC III	8.3	0.26	0.29	0.03

*values rounded, rel. Distribution represent values normalized between zero and one

Table 5.3.: Comparison of Metric and Survey Results

The other values range in between. Table 5.3 subsumes the survey complexity results C_S, the relative distribution of C_M and C_S and additionally the difference D of C_M* and C_S*. As shown in Table 5.3 the difference D of C_M and C_S is negligible.

In conclusion, the presented metric offers traceable results for evaluating the complexity of models developed with graphical modeling languages such as UML-diagrams, EPC, BPMN, ER-diagrams.

The metric calculates complexity of models developed with different process based and structure based modeling languages. In the forthcoming survey it is assumed that model complexity acts as a significant impact factor and, therefore, the impact on the survey output has to be controlled.

5.7. Conclusion

This developed metric aims for supporting empirical surveys on modeling languages. Therefore a metric analyzing and comparing complexity of models developed with different process and structure modeling languages was proposed.

It is important to consider semantic spread and connectivity degree in addition to model size. Considering generality of this approach it is important to mention some restrictions: To ensure generality this problem was solved on an abstract graph-based level. It is obvious that an EPC-event, UML-activity and UML-class are semantically different and cannot be compared by implication.

Hence, the proposed metric was built up focusing on graph theory i.e. nodes and edges. Subsequently, the development was influenced by moving from an abstract level to a concrete level adding semantic spread. Typical application domains for this metric are empirical surveys on modeling languages including model complexity. Another domain is the practical application of the proposed metric in organizations.

Currently organizations are designing process and structure models without considering model complexity and understandability. As a result, it may happen that simple business cases are modelled in a complex and unsuitable way. This leads to lower understandability and higher maintenance costs in an organization. Applying this metric might result in transparent models that are easy to understand for interpreting users. The developed metric is evaluated and applied in the empirical surveys in this thesis.

6. Comparing the Usability of Graphical Modeling Languages Using FUEML

Documenting, specifying and analyzing complex domains such as information systems or business processes have become unimaginable without the support of graphical models. Generally, models are developed using graph-oriented languages such as Event Driven Process Chains (EPC) or diagrams of the Unified Modeling Language (UML). For industrial use, modeling languages aim to describe either information systems or business processes. Heterogeneous modeling languages allow different grades of usability to their users. In the following chapter an evaluation of four heterogeneous modeling languages and their different impact on user performance and user satisfaction is conducted [Schalles et al., 2012]. The evaluation is based on the FUEML framework, which was developed in chapter 4 of this thesis.

Almost all notations for software and business process specifications use diagrams as the primary basis for documenting and communicating them. The large number of available languages confronts companies with the problem of selecting the language most suitable to their needs.

Beside functional and technical evaluation criteria, user-oriented characteristics of modeling languages are becoming more and more a focal point of interest in research and industry (Siau and Wang 2007).

In the following chapter a comparative study on usability of selected modeling languages is conducted. The remainder of this chapter is structured as follows: First, hypotheses that are relevant for analyzing the usability of modeling languages are defined. Secondly, the research methodology and design are introduced. Subsequently, the resulting empirical findings are presented. Based on the empirical results implications for different application domains of graphical modeling languages are deduced.

6.1. Underlying Hypotheses

Mayer (1989) defined three components acting as fundamental parts in the process of human performance from explanative information such as modeling languages connected with scenarios to be modelled and interpreted [Mayer, 1989]:

1. The content of particular scenarios to be modelled/interpreted
2. The capabilities of the modeling language to depict the content
3. The individual characteristics of the person applying the modeling language

Considering this in the following survey leads to the definition of several control variables. The objective is to compare and analyze language-based usability values and therefore, item (2) is focused on. Consequently, results are adjusted for model complexity (1) and user experience (3). The following section shows the underlying hypotheses supported by theory.

HYPOTHESIS 1. Process Modeling Languages are more usable than System Development Languages

In general, usability means focusing on users and especially behavioral aspects [Nielsen, 2006a]. It is hypothesized that languages applied for business process modeling result in higher usability values than languages applied for developing the conceptual design of application systems. Theoretical foundation of this hypothesis can be found in neuroscience and psychological research.

Neuroscience research found out that typically, subjects show a processing advantage for concrete concepts over abstract concepts [Crutch and Warrington, 2005].

The reason for that lies in the fact that abstract concepts lacking the direct sensory referents of concrete concepts [Paivio, 1986].

Additionally, subjects have a greater availability of contextual information in the knowledge base for concrete concepts [Schwanenflugel and Shoben, 1983].

For the domain of graphical modeling languages can be deduced that users of process modeling languages have greater availability of contextual information due to concrete imagination of tasks and similarities to familiar domains.

Additionally, further theoretic background from cognitive load theory can be introduced [Plass et al., 2010, Sweller, 2005].

The intrinsic cognitive load is determined by information complexity and interaction. For example, learning elements of modeling languages results in a low intrinsic cognitive load. In this case, the difficulty of learning a language and consequently the intrinsic cognitive load is strongly connected with the range of elements a language consists of. Contrariwise, the element interaction by means of syntactical and semantic element relations leads to a high intrinsic cognitive load. Consequently, the syntactical complexity of modeling languages highly determines the cognitive load. For example, a class diagram of the UML consists of various different relations such as generalization, aggregation, composition etc. set between classes. Due to this, the element interaction is much higher compared to control flows and object flows in process modeling languages. It is generally stated, that this issue determines the usability of graphical modeling languages and subsequently leads to different usability values between process and system development languages.

HYPOTHESIS 2. Behavioral Languages are more usable than Structural Languages

In general, this hypothesis builds on H1. The OMG structures the languages of the UML in (a) behavioral and (2) structural languages [OMG, 2005a]. H2 assumes that users are more familiar with behavioral languages such as UML Activity Diagrams or UML Use Case Diagrams due to concrete imagination of tasks to be modelled or interpreted compared to structural diagrams such as UML Class Diagrams. It is assumed that this fact leads to different usability values between behavioral and structural languages.

HYPOTHESIS 3. Complex Languages are not as usable as simple structured Languages

This hypothesis is deduced from the observation that humans have limited cognitive capacity [Siau and Wang, 2007, Gemino and Wand, 2004].

It is presumed that more complex languages are harder to absorb and understand in the human's brain than models with less complexity [Recker and Dreiling, 2007].

The rationale for this observation is quite obvious. Consequently, it is stated that languages with high complexity result in low usability values compared to languages offering low complexity.

HYPOTHESIS 4. Languages offering high visual differentiation are more usable than languages offering low visual differentiation

In the modeling language domain visual differentiation is strongly connected with the number of different element colors and geometric element shapes set in the specification of the modeling language [Schalles et al., 2011b]. Hall and Hanna (2004) analyzed the impact of color on web usability attributes in an empirical survey. They concluded that the application of different colors results in a higher grade of website structuredness, which leads to more efficient information processing in the user's brain [Hall and Hanna, 2004].

Moody and Heymans (2010) found out that visual differentiation of language properties impact on cognitive effectiveness in practical usage scenarios. Transferring this leads to the assumption that more element colors set in the language's metamodel lead to more information structuredness, which supports the usability of modeling languages. Furthermore, it is assumed that the variance of different geometric shapes depicting different element types is positively influencing information processing in the user's brain [Moody and Heymans, 2010] .

The theoretical basis for this assumption is initially given by Comber and Maltby (1997). They concluded that screen complexity including the application of various geometric shapes is a positive influencing variable of usability [Comber and Maltby, 1997].

Consequently, all these theoretical findings lead to the hypothesis, that languages offering high visual differentiation are more usable than languages offering low visual differentiation.

	Context of Use	Modeling Concept	Language Complexity	Degree of different Geometrics*	Degree of different Colors**
EPC	Business Process Modeling	behavioral	19.26	1.00	0.80
UML Activity Diagrams	Software Engineering	behavioral	11.18	0.75	0.25
UML Class Diagrams	Software Engineering	structural	26.40	0.86	0.29
UML Use Case Diagrams	Software Engineering	behavioral	10.39	0.33	0.33

*   Values taken from Table 4.1
**   Number of different shapes/total number of different elements
*** Number of different element colors/total number of different elements

Table 6.1.: Chosen Modeling Languages

6.2. Survey Design and Data Collection

This study uses a large set of various data collection methods for measuring the different usability variables. Furthermore, two data collection sessions per modeling language are introduced. The data collection focused on model development and model interpretation tasks. Within these sessions error rates, grades of completeness and task finishing times for calculating efficiency, effectiveness and learnability, which is the relative learning growth between two data collection sessions are collected.

Additionally, the method of eye tracking for analyzing visual perceptibility of modeling languages specifically for the model interpretation scenario is applied. The instruments were either adapted from traditional usability research or new measurement items focusing on modeling languages were developed.

A pretest was conducted prior collecting data for the field test. All pilot test participants were excluded from the analysis sample.

The data collection was based on two different modeling concepts and connected languages. On the one hand process based languages, Event driven Process Chains (EPC), UML Activity Diagrams and on the other hand structure based modeling languages, UML Use Case and UML Class Diagrams. These languages were chosen due to their cross-variability concerning the context of use, modeling concept, language complexity and visual properties.

For measuring learnability a second measuring point was introduced.

The first part of each session focused on model development based on a given scenario described

Figure 6.2.1.: Tobii Eye Tracker T60

textually. For model development the Bflow*-toolbox[1] and ArgoUML[2] modeling tools were applied. Those two modeling tools are quite similar and offer a drawing area and a general overview of all elements of one specific modeling language. It is assumed that the modeling tools might have a significant influence on the usability metrics, however, the aim of this study is to analyze and to compare the usability of modeling languages. Since the design of the two modeling tools applied is quite similar, the values of this study are comparable.

In the second part the participants were confronted with the interpretation of given models. The interpretation scenario was structured in two parts. The first part was focusing on general observation while the second part included verbal interpretation of given models. Data was collected by using Tobii Eye Tracker T60[3] integrated a webcam and a microphone.

However, the interpretation task generates time, error, completeness and additionally eye tracking values. At the beginning of second data collection phase the knowledge tests for measuring the ability of remembering specific metalevel properties were distributed. Subsequently, the User Satisfaction Questionnaire was administered to the participants. Figure 6.2 shows the overall procedure of data collection.

6.2.1. Measurement Scales

The general usability measurement method in this section is based on the framework for usability evaluation of modeling languages (FUEML) [Schalles et al., 2010a]. FUEML proposes the differentiation of evaluation procedure in usability attributes specified for each model development

---

[1]http://www.bflow.org
[2]http://www.argouml.tigris.org
[3]http://www.tobii.com

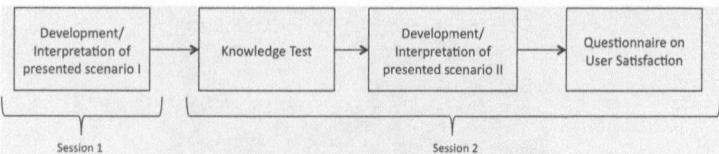

Figure 6.2.2.: Procedure of the Data Collection Phase

and model interpretation scenarios. Furthermore, the framework contains metrics for measuring and comparing the resulting values germane to all graphical modeling languages. The concrete development and interpretation tasks are shown in the appendix A.1. of this thesis.

6.2.2. Sample

The sample includes second year students of business informatics. The experimental data collection, the questionnaire and the knowledge test were conducted with these students. The overall sample size amounts 114 students, 47% female and 53% male.

Even though a choice of students for experiments has sometimes been criticized for lack of external validity, it is agreed with Gemino and Wand (2004) and Batra et al. (1992). They confirmed that the selection of students over practitioners could in fact be advisable [Gemino and Wand, 2004, Batra and Davis, 1992].

Participants that are able to bring to bear prior knowledge in software and process engineering are sufficient for analyzing human impact criteria in the domain of graphical modeling languages [Siau and Loo, 2006].

Hence, the selection of students overcomes the problem of controlling for any bias in technique or domain familiarity.

6.3. Data Analysis

The hypotheses testing was completed using an analysis of covariance (ANCOVA) technique. In general, ANCOVA is used to adjust for difference between categories influenced by another variable called the covariate. In this study ANCOVA is primarily used to calculate the estimated means. ANCOVA allows to remove covariates form the list of possible explanations of variance in the dependent variable. ANCOVA is used in experimental studies when researchers want to remove the effects of some antecedent variable [Vogt, 1999].

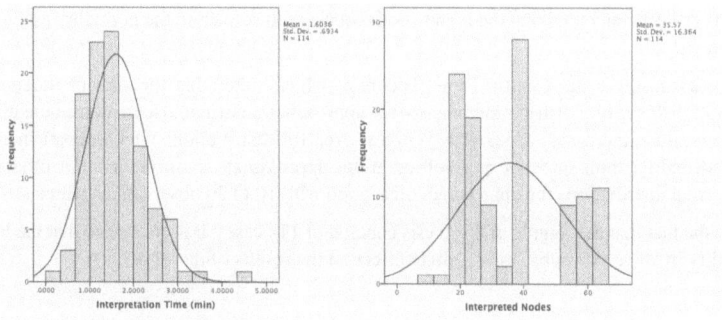

Figure 6.3.1.: Histograms Plot with Normal Curve

With calculating the estimated means the influence of the covariate is partialled out. Concerning this, the covariates are user's general modeling experience, language experience and task complexity.

The aim of this analysis is to determine whether there is a statistically significant difference between EPCs, UML Activity Diagrams, UML Class Diagrams and UML Use Case Diagrams impacting on defined usability attributes considering user experience and task complexity as covariates. The ANCOVA including the analysis of the adjusted means was conducted using the statistical software package SPSS 19.

For calculating an ANCOVA, the dataset has to meet several assumptions that are analyzed in the following section:

6.3.1. Normal Distribution

A general assumption of the ANCOVA is that the variables of the population are normal distributed. All residuals were tested for normality using Kolmogorov-Smirnov-z values. Several variables such as the number of interpreted nodes seem to be not normal distributed.

Figure 6.3.1 shows two variables of the sample distributed unevenly. Statistics literature recommend the normal distribution as an assumption for calculating an ANCOVA [Dancey and Reidy, 2011].

However, numerous studies have examined the effect of violations of assumptions in ANCOVA, and an excellent summary of this literature has been provided by Glass, Peckham, and Sanders (1972). Their review indicates that non-normality has only a slight effect on the type I error rate, even for very skewed or kurtotic distributions [Glass et al., 1972].

Stevens (1999) concluded that the F-statistic is robust with respect to the normality assumption [Stevens, 1999].

The basic reason is the Central Limit Theorem, which states that the sum of independent observations have any distribution whatsoever approaches a normal distribution as the number of observations increases. Bock (1975) notes, even for distributions which depart markedly from normality, sums of 50 or more observations approximate to normality. For moderately non-normal distributions the approximation is good with 10 to 20 observations [Bock, 1975].

Due to the fact that the sample in this thesis concsist of 114 cases, it is concluded that the lack of normality in all variables has only a slight effect on the results of the ANCOVA.

6.3.2. Interaction Effects

Furthermore, the interaction effect of the variables was analyzed. Variables interact if the effect of one of the variables differs depending on the level of the other variable [Dancey and Reidy, 2011]. The analysis of the interaction effects between all independent variables and covariates resulted in insignificant values. Consequently, no variable interaction between independent variables was detected.

6.3.3. Missing Data

As the research instrument of this study contains several collection methods such as questionnaire, knowledge test and empirical tasks the possibility of missing data seems to be reasonable. Therefore, the dataset was analyzed regarding missing values. The rate of missing values in the dataset is less than two percent. For dealing with missing values the multiple imputation method offered by SPSS 19 was chosen.

Multiple imputation accounts for missing data by restoring not only the natural variability in the data, but also by incorporating the incertainty caused by estimating missing data. The performance of multiple imputation in a variety of missing data situations has been well-studied and it has been shown to perform favorably [Schafer and Graham, 2002].

6.3.4. Methodology of the Data Analysis

The data analysis was conducted in the following steps [Dancey and Reidy, 2011]:

1. Calculation of the estimated means for each variable

2. Conduction of the Levene's test (F-measure and significance level) for each variable

3. Calculation of the FUEML usability metrics applying the estimated means

4. Conduction of the Levene's test for each usability metric

A detailed result overview showing Levene's test per variable is shown in appendix section A.2. (online supplement). In the following table an aggregation of the results calculated by applying the metrics of the evaluation framework FUEML is presented. The values for User Satisfaction and Memorability were normalized between 0 and 1 and are based on the arithmetic mean of particular questionnaire and knowledge test items shown in detail in the appendix section A.2.

		EPC	UML Activity Diagram	UML Use Case Diagram	UML Class Diagram
Language Complexity		19.26	11.18	10.39	26.40
Visual Differentiation	Geometrics*	1.00	0.75	0.33	0.86
	Colors**	0.80	0.25	0.33	0.29
Effectiveness (=Grade of completeness*Grade of correctness)	Development (p=0.007), (F=4.231)	**0.943******	0.897	0.912	0.836
	Interpretation (p=0.000), (F=7.463)	**0.983**	0.970	0.891	0.882
Efficiency (=Effectiveness/Task time***)	Development (p=0.071) (F=2.405)	0.074	**0.099**	0.051	0.033
	Interpretation (p=0.046), (F=2.466)	0.411	**0.438**	0.382	0.321
Learnability (=Rise of Efficiency in% between Session 1 and Session 2)	Development (p=0.042), (F=5.236)	**121.134**	13.549	45.576	116.469
	Interpretation (p=0.024), (F=6.563)	45.267	0.294	**63.321**	-8.422
Memorability (Normalized between 0 and 1)	Both Development and Interpretation (p=0.000), (F=18.255)	0.804	0.600	**0.815**	0.496
User Satisfaction (Normalized between 0 and 1)	General Impression (p=0.000), (F=8.947)	**0.734**	0.679	0.649	0.577
	Development (p=0.017), (F=3.540)	**0.748**	0.717	0.704	0.614
	Interpretation (p=0.037) (F=4.789)	**0.786**	0.777	0.749	0.734
Perceptibility (Information search=Fixation count) (Information extraction=fixation Duration)	Interpretation (p=0.000), (F=19.971) Information Search	**111.000**	188.000	153.000	248.000
	Interpretation (p=0.001), (F=8.768) Information Extraction	97.920	74.280	84.570	**73.870**

Note. All shown values are significant at least at the 0.05 level. Additional information for Significance and F-values are presented in appendix. Bold values show best language results for each usability attribute.
* Number of different shapes/total number of different elements
** Number of different element colors/total number of different elements
*** Value taken from Appendix
****Values represent adjusted means

Table 6.2.: ANCOVA Results for Usability Attributes across heterogeneous Modeling Languages

6.3.5. Hypotheses Testing

In the following chapter the hypotheses of the study are proved by analyzing the results of the ANCOVA.

Hypothesis H1 is mostly confirmed:

H1 hypothesized that business process modeling languages are more usable than system development modeling languages. This hypothesis is supported by our empirical results mostly. As well in development as in interpretation scenarios, EPCs are the most effective modeling language in this survey. Furthermore, UML Activity Diagrams are most efficient in development and interpretation scenarios.

Thus, this is not contributing to H1, since an Activity Diagram is a specific UML-language for depicting application system processes. However, the fact that EPCs are more efficient than UML Use Case and UML Class Diagrams is supporting this hypothesis. In most cases, the learnability of EPCs in model development scenarios is higher compared to the other modeling languages analyzed in this survey. In model interpretation scenarios the learnability is best with UML Use Case Diagrams.

Concerning the memorability of different language properties and the particular application, UML Use Case Diagrams fits best. Users are most satisfied with applying EPCs in model development and model interpretation scenarios. Furthermore, searching for information is most efficient in EPC diagrams. However, the extraction of information is obviously most efficient in UML Class Diagrams.

In conclusion, H1 is somewhat supported for model interpretation scenarios. However, H1 is strongly supported for model development scenarios. Overall, H1 is mostly supported for model development scenarios by the empirical results.

Hypothesis H2 is strongly confirmed:

H2 stated that behavioral languages are more usable than structural languages. Considering the results, it is concluded that H2 is fully supported except the information extraction variable in interpretation scenarios.

The results show a processing advantage for concrete concepts over abstract concepts for the domain of graphical modeling languages [Crutch and Warrington, 2005]. Considering usability, the issue of language abstraction seems to be of a great significance for the domain of graphical modeling languages.

Furthermore, it is verified that users of process modeling languages have greater availability of contextual information due to concrete imagination of tasks and similarities to familiar domains such as business processes and specific process steps. Consequently, it can be concluded that the grade of formalization of a graphical modeling language influences the usability of this language negatively.

Hypothesis H3 is partly confirmed:

H3 assumes that complex languages are not as usable as simple structured languages. This hypothesis is partly confirmed by the results. For example, class diagrams (complexity=26.40) are comparable complex and the results show that they are not as usable as EPCs (complexity=19.26), UML Activity Diagrams (complexity=11.18) and UML Use Case Diagrams (complexity=10.39).

So far, this fact supports this hypothesis. However, EPCs are more usable than UML Activity Diagrams and UML Use Case Diagrams. Although, they consist of more elements, relations and properties i.e. they are more complex.

Hypothesis H4 is fully confirmed:

H4 presumes that languages, which offer a high visual differentiation, are more usable than languages offering low visual differentiation. This hypothesis is confirmed by the empirical results. EPCs, which offer the highest visual differentiation in the metamodel, are the most usable language in this survey.

6.4. Discussion

With the exception of H4, the results for H1-H3 are indeed surprising because it is not possible to confirm or delete a hypothesis with 100 percent. As shown in Table 6.2 every language has advantages in usability results on the attribute level. For example, EPCs are the most usable language for model development scenarios whereas UML Class Diagrams have high values in extracting information out of models in model interpretation scenarios. This leads to the first deduction from the empirical results.

Languages influence usability on the attribute level

It becomes obvious that it is not possible to calculate a single usability measure for evaluating modeling languages. The results show that different languages have different advantages and disadvantages on the usability attribute level. This finding is contributing to conclusions of Birkmeier et al. (2010). They conducted a survey including EPC and UML Activity Diagrams on selected usability measures. Their general conclusion was that it is not possible to make general recommendations. Rather, it comes clear that different modeling languages have advantages or disadvantages regarding different usability attributes [Birkmeier et al., 2010].

Separation between development and interpretation scenarios

The results confirm the strict separation between model development and model interpretation scenarios proposed in the usability evaluation framework (FUEML) underlying this survey

(Schalles et al. 2010b). For example, UML Class Diagrams, and EPCs have a comparable learnability in model development scenarios. Contrariwise, the learnability of these languages is significantly less in model interpretation scenarios.

Behavioral languages are more usable than structural languages

For almost all usability attributes the results are headed by behavioral languages. The empirical results confirm that behavioral modeling languages result in higher measuring values concerning the different usability attributes than structural modeling languages. Obviously, human beings show a neuro-processing advantage for concrete concepts over abstract concepts [Crutch and Warrington, 2005].

Transferring this into the domain of graphical modeling languages leads to the conclusion that users of behavioral modeling languages have greater availability of contextual information (i.e. concrete imagination, similarities etc.) compared to structural modeling languages. This is extended by the fact, that EPCs show high usability in many attributes. From this can be deduced, that process modeling is more usable than system modeling due to different abstraction levels. Additionally, the results show that languages offering low complexity result in high values indicating memorability. This finding is contributing to Kintsch (1998), who shows that cognitive processes underlie the comprehension of a specific domain [Kintsch, 1998].

Language usability is influencd by language complexity and visual differentiation set in the metamodel

Nembhard and Napassavong (2002) found out that the complexity of a specific domain influences memorability negatively [Nembhard and Napassavong, 2002]. Since our results contribute to the intrinsic Cognitive Load, this fact underlines the application of Cognitive Load Theory in usability assessment of graphical modeling languages. The results indicate that languages offering visual differentiation in the metamodel are generally more usable than languages offering low visual differentiation. This contributes to the extraneous cognitive load, which is influenced by the way the information is represented [Sweller, 2005]. These results underline findings of Moody and Hillegersberg (2009). They found out, that increasing visual differentiation in language specifications could optimize the visual effectiveness and consequently the visual perceptibility of graphical modeling languages [Moody and Hillegersberg, 2009].

The search for information in diagrams developed by using specific languages is most efficient in EPC diagrams. A probable reason for this may be due to the fact that the specification and the metamodel of EPCs strictly set the use of different colors and different shapes for particular elements. Accordingly, the information structuredness in EPC diagrams is higher compared to UML Activity, UML Use Case and UML Class Diagrams leading to more efficient information search procedures in model interpretation scenarios [Hall and Hanna, 2004].

Contrariwise, the extraction of information out of class diagrams is easier compared to EPCs, UML Activity and UML Use Case Diagrams. However, at this stage it is essential to consider the quality of information extraction.

With comparing the values for effectiveness it is concluded that information extraction out of class diagrams is comparable easy but the quality of information extraction is comparable low. A possible reason for that lies in the fact that the size of UML Class Diagrams is comparable low in relation to information density. This increases the efficiency of information extraction. Indeed, the information density in UML Class Diagrams is comparable higher than the density of information in EPCs, UML Activity Diagrams and UML Use Case Diagrams. This is based on the fact that UML Class Diagrams consist of comparable less elements and relations. But various properties such as multiplicities can be added to them resulting in a higher grade of variation. This fact lets class diagrams appear more difficult to use than EPCs, UML Activity Diagrams and UML Use Case Diagrams.

Users have preferences for process modeling languages

Furthermore, the results imply that users prefer process modeling languages for modeling and interpreting scenarios. On the one hand we suppose that this behavior is based on the fact that process modeling languages are comparable less complex and easy to understand due to greater availability of contextual and concrete information [Schwanenflugel and Shoben, 1983].

UML Activity Diagrams offer greater task efficiency than EPCs

Another interesting finding is that UML Activity Diagrams support most efficient task accomplishment in the survey in model development as well as model interpretation scenarios. A possible reason might be that they are not as complex as EPCs. For example, UML Activity Diagrams include the swim lane concept for adding information about specific task (=activity) responsibilities whereas EPCs need the organizational unit for every task (=function). This increases the visual spread of an EPC-diagram significantly.

6.5. Implications

The implications that can be deduced from our results give insights into

- Modeling and Education,
- Modeling Language Development and
- Business Process Modeling.

6.5.1. Modeling in Education

Within the scope of this study it could mostly be confirmed that business process modeling languages are more usable than system development languages. What does that imply for educational usage of modeling languages? First, it is recommended that training courses on modeling languages for software development should be more intensive than courses on business process modeling languages. This recommendation focuses on the pure training with the modeling language with the exception of tool and domain influences.

The results confirm that different modeling concepts have different impact on the usability and consisting attributes. Furthermore, it is confirmed that behavioral languages are more usable than structural languages. Again, this implies that structural modeling languages such as the UML Class Diagram need more educational language-based training intensity than behavioral languages.

6.5.2. Modeling Language Development

An interesting implication could be deduced concerning the use of EPCs or UML Activity Diagrams for modeling real-world scenarios. EPCs are more usable than UML Activity Diagrams. This result is tracked back on the fact that EPCs support visual differentiation due to the use of various colors and geometric shapes in the language specification. Consequently, the usability-oriented optimization of UML might be reached by adding different colors and different shapes. This implication coincides with findings of Moody and Heymans (2010) [Moody and Heymans, 2010].

Additionally, the results imply that UML Activity Diagrams support more efficient task accomplishments in model development and model interpretation scenarios. Obviously, activity diagrams allow users fast model development and model interpretation procedures. A possible reason is the low language complexity of Activity diagrams compared to EPCs. However, this issue is only partly considered in the new BPMN 2.0 release of the Object Management Group in January 2011. For example, with this new release the BPMN was extended with plenty of technical extensions.

Though, additional visual differentiations (i.e. colors, geometric shapes etc.) were not added yet. Looking at another major language, the UML 2.0, the situation is quite equivalent. It seems, that language specification organizations focus on technical language optimization whereas the human being acting as user is partly ignored in those optimizing activities.

This empirical study shows that it could be worth thinking about usability-related topics in further development of graphical modeling languages.

6.5.3. Business Process Modeling

The results show that EPCs, a language for modeling business processes, offer the best usability in this survey. In companies the importance of business process modeling has steadily risen. Consequently, the development and interpretation of models become an issue of organizational concerns. How efficiently can models be developed or interpreted?

For the model interpretation scenario, questions such as whether employees understand the information modelled do appear. Thus, companies aiming for fast, complete and correct model interpretation, e.g. business process consulting companies, typically apply modeling languages offering high variability in visual properties. In many cases those companies customize languages such as the BPMN by adding colors or shapes to support complete and accurate model interpretation.

Since EPCs offer highest usability values in development and interpretation scenarios, our results support this course of action. Further studies are required for analyzing language-based impacting factors of different usability attributes in this domain.

6.6. Conclusion

The results imply deeper potential for analyzing the usability of modeling languages. In this chapter a comparison of different selected modeling languages and their impact of usability attributes was conducted. What is missing yet, are the impacting characteristics on usability in the domain of graphical modeling languages specifically.

This could be very interesting for defining recommendations focusing on further development of existing modeling languages. Thus, a further inductive, causal study is conducted in the following chapters to bring out new and important findings of how language specific criteria impact on usability attributes on different causal stages.

7. Using Structural Equation Modeling in Usability Research

The following two chapters extend the empirical analysis of chapter six by analyzing language's metaproperties and their causal impact on different usability attributes. The findings show how the metaproperties of modeling languages influence usability and connected attributes. Chapter seven introduces a statistical methodology for detecting and analyzing causal interactions [Schalles et al., 2011a].

In the area of usability research structural equation models have not been applied intensely. A possible reason for that might be the fact that principles of usability theory are gradually making their way to the mainstream software applications but the underlying research is less known [Ilomäki, 2008].

With this chapter the statistic concept of Structural Equation Modeling (SEM) is introduced. Furthermore, a suitable algorithm for the SEM for calculating SEMs is derived. Additionally, a method for using SEM in usability research is proposed.

The findings of this chapter are essential for the empirical analysis conducted in chapter eight of this thesis.

7.1. Structural Equation Modeling

SEM is a statistical approach, which focuses on testing hypotheses and consequently analyzing of a structural theory bearing on some phenomenon [Kline, 2005].

Particular theory represents causal interactions that generate observations on multiple latent variables. The specialty of latent variables is caused by non-direct measurability.

Consequently, latent variable analysis is only possible with defining indicating variables (i.e. manifest variables) for establishing an empirical relationship.

7.1.1. Fundamentals of Structural Equation Modeling

The term "structural equation modeling" transfers two essential aspects of this procedure: First, the causal processes under study are represented by a series of structural equations. Secondly,

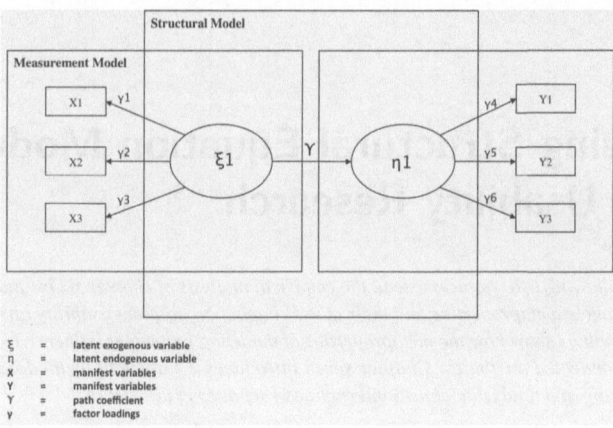

Figure 7.1.1.: General SEM Structure

these structural relations can be modelled graphically to enable a clearer conceptualization of the theory under study.

Subsequently, the hypothesized model can be tested statistically in a simultaneous analysis of the entire system of variables to determine the extent to which it is consistent with the data. If goodness of fit is adequate, the model argues for the plausibility of postulated relations among variables; if it is inadequate, the tenability of such relations is rejected.

In general, a structural equation model consists of (1) structural relations between latent variables and (2) indicating variables for measuring latent constructs. subsection 7.1.1 shows the general structure of a structural equation model.

The measurement model formulation depends on the direction of the relationships between the latent variables and the corresponding manifest variables
[Fornell and Bookstein, 1982]. Consequently, two different types of measurement models are available: the reflective model and the formative model.

In a reflective model the block of manifest variables related to a latent variable is assumed to measure a unique underlying concept. Each manifest variable reflects the corresponding latent variable and plays a role of endogenous variable in the block specific measurement model.

In the formative model, each manifest variable or each sub block of manifest variables represents a different dimension of the underlying concept. Therefore, unlike the reflective model, the formative model does not assume homogeneity nor unidimensionality of the block. The latent variable is defined as a linear combination of the corresponding manifest variables, thus each manifest variable is an exogenous variable in the measurement model.

7.1.2. Assumptions of Structural Equation Modeling

SEM is a flexible and powerful extension of the general linear model. Like any statistical method, it features a number of assumptions. These assumptions should be met or at least approximated to ensure reliable results.

Reasonable sample size

According to Stevens (2001) a good rule of thumb is 15 cases per predictor in a standard ordinary least squares multiple regression analysis [Stevens, 2001]. Actually, the assumptions for the sample size are influenced by the algorithm chosen for model calculation. An intensive discussion on SEM calculation algorithms is offered in chapter 7.1.3 of this thesis.

Continuously and normally distributed endogenous variables

One of the most important assumptions for SEM is that the variables follow a normal distribution. The normality assumption in SEM applies to all observed variables [Blanthorne et al.,]. However, this assumptions is strongly dependend on the specific algorithm chosen for the calculation of the structural equation model. For a more detailed discussion on that topic see chapter 7.1.3.

Complete data or appropriate handling of incomplete data

In educational and social science research it is impossible to collect data that is complete. For example, when administering a survey participants may answer some questions and not others. This missing data causes a problem for researchers using SEM techniques for data analysis. Because SEM and multivariate methods require complete data, several methods such as the casewise deletion, pairwise deletion and the imputation have been proposed for dealing with missing data [Lynn, 2006]. At last, appropriate handling methods are offered in most SEM calculation tools and additionally in statistics software such as SPSS 19.

Theoretical basis for model specification and causality

Generally, SEM needs a strong theoretical basis for the development of the structural and the measurement model. Famous SEM calculation algorithms such as LISREL meet the assumption for a strong theoretical basis in the developed structural equation model. However, algorithms offering less assumptions on the theoretical basis do exist. The Partial Least Squares (PLS) method comes into the process of theory construction at an early stage when theories have not been developed or adapted sufficiently to propose causal relationships [Wallenburg and Weber, 2005].

7.1.3. Alternative SEM calculation techniques: LISREL versus PLS

In recent years, two competing algorithms for calculating SEM models have gained importance: linear structural relations (LISREL) based on covariance structure analysis and Partial Least Squares (PLS) [Henseler et al., 2009].

Developed mainly by Joreskog (1978), the covariance structure analysis is a causal analytical approach, which is often termed LISREL [Jöreskog, 1978]. Even though LISREL represents the dominant method for SEM, in recent years the alternative approach offered by PLS path modeling has increasingly received attention for the analysis of latent variables in structural equation models [Chin, 1998, Tenenhaus et al., 2005]. Based on a comparison of PLS and LISREL, as illustrated in Table 7.1, reasons are given for applying the PLS approach as a SEM method in usability research.

The first argument for utilizing PLS is that LISREL aims to minimize the difference between the covariances of an empirical sample and those predicted by a theoretical model [Chin, 1998]. Therefore, the parameter estimation process intends to most closely reproduce the covariance matrix of the empirically observed measures [Chin and Newsted, 1999].

The objective of PLS is prediction. Based on an analysis of the raw data matrix, the parameter estimation process of PLS aims to obtain the best weight estimates for each block of indicators that correspond to each latent variable [Chin, 1998].

This explorative character of PLS is in contrast to the confirmative approach of LISREL, which tests the validity of a priori defined models [Tenenhaus et al., 2005]. Thus, LISREL is more adequate for causal model/theory testing, while PLS is more appropriate for component-based predictive modeling [Wold, 1980, Henseler et al., 2009].

In usability research, a strong theory is missing yet. PLS has much lower requirements on prior theoretical knowledge than LISREL. Consequently, PLS allows the confirmation of unknown relationships that have been defined solely on the basis of plausible hypotheses [Chin and Newsted, 1999, Henseler et al., 2009]. Due to this, PLS seems to be more suitable than LISREL in usability research. Furthermore, LISREL requires a multivariate normal distribution of the data, that the observations are independent of each other and a large sample size. In contrast, PLS does not require a normal distribution of manifest variables, as its parameter estimations are based solely on the regression principle.

Additionally, minimal recommendations in PLS for the size of the research sample range from 30 to 100 cases. The latter range of participants seems more realistic for the sample in usability research. Due to survey complexity, it is not expected to reach the minimum sample size in

Criteria	LISREL	PLS
Methodology	Covariance-based	Variance-based
Main objective	Parameter oriented: Explanation of empirical data structures	Prediction oriented: Explanation of latent and manifest variables
Implication	Optimal for parameter accuracy	Optimal for prediction accuracy
Theory requirements	High	Flexible
Assumptions	Multivariate normal distribution and independent observations	Predictor specification
Measurement Model	Reflective	Reflective and/or formative
Sample Size	Large sample size (minimum recommendations reach from 200 to 800 cases)	Also appropriate for small sample sizes (minimum recommendation reach from 30 to 100 cases)

Table 7.1.: Comparison of LISREL and PLS [Chin and Newsted, 1999, Fornell and Bookstein, 1982]

LISREL of 200 cases in usability research and consequently for the survey conducted in this thesis. Table 7.1 shows a detailed comparison of LISREL and PLS.

7.2. A Methodology for Applying SEM in Usability Research

This chapter offer a deduced methodological proposal for applying SEM in the domain of usability research. In the first step usability is operationalized for supporting measurability. Second, the structural model including structural causal relations is produced. And third, the model quality is assessed by applying statistical quality measures for both the measurement model and the structural model.

7.2.1. Operationalization of Usability for SEM-Use

First, usability has to be made measurable by

- defining usability attributes and
- developing metrics for measuring different attributes.

7.2.1.1. Definition of Attributes defining Usability

The usability concept in the domain of graphical modeling languages is specified in the FUEML framework by

- Learnability,
- Memorability,
- Effectiveness,
- Efficiency and
- User Satisfaction [Schalles et al., 2010a].

In the special case of the model interpretation scenario the attribute of

- Visual Perceptibility

is introduced.

The proposition is that these attributes and especially their causal interaction influence the usability of modeling languages.

7.2.1.2. Measurement of Usability Attributes

The general development of metrics for measuring usability attributes in the modeling domain are proposed in the developed FUEML framework (see chapter 4). For reasons of transparency and readability the following section subsumes the most important findings for measuring different usability attributes.

Evaluating *effectiveness* requires analysis of task output with measuring quantity and quality of goal achievement [Rengger et al., 1993]. Quantity is defined as the proportion of task goals represented in the output of a task. Quality is the degree to which the task goals represented in the output have been achieved [Bevan, 1995]. Bevan (1995) defined effectiveness as a product of quantity and quality. Transferring this, indicating manifest variables for measuring effectiveness are the grade of completeness and the grade of correctness of a task conducted in usability experiments.

The *efficiency* is the amount of human, economical and temporal resources. Measures of efficiency relate to the level of effectiveness achieved to the expenditure of resources [Bevan, 1995]. Measure values of efficiency include time taken to complete tasks, i.e. duration time for performing an experimental task [Vuolle et al., 2008]. Learnability describes the ease of learning the application of applications, devices or websites. For this characteristic, the standard measure values are based on task completion rates and the task accuracy [Seffah et al., 2006]. In general, learnability is a development and can be graphically described by learning curves [Tamir et al., 2008].

Hence, *learnability* can be measured by the rate of difference when the user repeats evaluation sessions [Bevan, 1995]. Nielsen (2006) insists that highly learnable systems could be categorized as "allowing users to reach a reasonable level of usage proficiency (...)" [Nielsen, 2006b]. Furthermore, Nielsen (2006) proposes measuring proficiency by quantity and quality and of task fulfilment. Thus, it is proposed choosing grade of completeness and grade of correctness as basic variables for measuring learnability. With conducting two measuring points mp and $mp+1$, it is possible to analyze the relative difference between mp and $mp+1$ for indicating Δ *learnability*, i.e. individual learning progress in percent [Nembhard and Napassavong, 2002, Grossman et al., 2009].

The *visual perceptibility* is measured by using the method of eye-tracking with analyzing the user's visual attention [Gordon, 2004]. In our research we aim to include eye-tracking for measuring user's cognitive processes i.e. information search and information extraction. The pioneering work regarding the use of eye-tracking was first carried out by Fitts et al. (1950). They proposed that fixation length is a measure of difficulty of information extraction and interpretation [Fitts et al., 1950]. Fixations are eye movements that stabilize the gaze over an object of interest. During this, the brain starts to process the visual information received from the eyes [Duchowski, 2007]. The number of fixations overall is thought to be negatively correlated with search efficiency [Goldberg and Kotval, 1999]. Consequently, a larger number of fixations indicates less efficient information search in a website etc. Furthermore, we aim to analyze the difficulty of information extraction out of devices, applications and websites. Byrne et al. (1999) propose tracking fixation duration time as a measure for information extraction [Byrne et al., 1999]. From this follows that longer fixations times indicate a participant's difficulty extracting information from a website etc.

Compared to the other attributes defining usability, the individual *satisfaction of a user* is a user subjective criterion that can be measured best by using standardized questionnaires [Vuolle et al., 2008]. Currently no unified standardized method for measuring user satisfaction does exist. Therefore, questionnaires focusing on system and website usability were adapted [Kirakowski and Corbett, 1993, Armstrong et al., 2005]. For evaluating user satisfaction a questionnaire, which consists of thirty items structured in 1) General impression, 2) Recommendation rate and 3) Language application was developed. The development of this questionnaire is generally contributing to the Questionnaire for User Interaction Satisfaction (QUIS) and additionally the Software Usability Measurement Inventory (SUMI) [Chin et al., 1988, Kirakowski and Corbett,

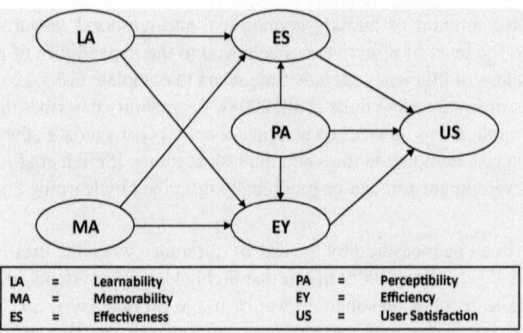

Figure 7.2.1.: Example of a Structural Model in Usability Research

1993].

Memorability is best measured as proficiency after a period of non-use provided a user has already learned a language [Olle et al., 1986, Seffah et al., 2006]. Accordingly, the measure values for memorability are neglect curves and time-delayed knowledge tests [Nembhard and Napassavong, 2002]. Concerning usability, the user must remember the different elements and its intended meaning (semantics), the syntax and the application. In due consideration of Nielsen (2006), the measuring points interval should be several weeks regarding memorability [Nielsen, 2006b].

7.2.2. Developing a Structural Model

Developing structural relations is the initial basis of structural equation modeling. The assumed causal relations should be based on (1) theory or (2) intrinsic logical reasons [Weiber and Mühlhaus, 2009]. Figure 7.2.1 shows a possible example of a structural model including latent variables and connecting causal relations in the usability domain. The relations are specified by hypotheses deduced from theory.[1]

Besides, the consideration of variables influencing causal relationships between latent variables is very important when developing the structural model. These effects are called moderating variables and they are evoked by variables whose variation influences the strength or the direction of a relationship between manifest variables.

---

[1] see chapter 8 of this thesis for a detailed description of the structural model development

Moderator variables can either be metric (e.g., user psychological constructs like experience or intelligence) or categorical (e.g., gender or education level) in nature. One example of the examination of moderating effects is a paper by [Homburg and Giering, 2001].

They find that age and income have significant effects on the strength of the relationship between customer satisfaction and customer loyalty. In that context, age and income serve as moderator variables. In usability context we found out that users of applications, websites etc. differ regarding their experience. This fact influences the task accomplishment and consequently the usability and has to be considered in a research model [Nielsen, 2006b].

Furthermore, when conducting a survey on usability evaluation, the complexity of particular tasks must be controlled and treated as moderator variables for minimizing its influence on the outcome.

7.2.3. Assessing Model Quality

The following assessment recommendations for model quality focus on the PLS-algorithm, which is applied for SEM calculation in the research presented in this thesis.

For ensuring reliability of causal estimations between different constructs in a structural model it is important to define and apply statistical quality criteria. Compared to LISREL-approach, PLS path modeling does not provide any global goodness-of-fit criteria. As a consequence, Chin (1998) has put forward a catalogue of criteria to assess partial model structures [Chin, 1998].

A systematic application of these criteria is a two-step process, encompassing

1. the assessment of the outer model and

2. the assessment of the inner model.

Concerning this, it is important to distinguish between reflective and formative measurement models.

Usually, the first criterion checked is internal consistency reliability. The traditional criterion for internal consistency is Cronbach's Alpha, which provides an estimate for the reliability based on the indicator intercorrelations [Cronbach, 1951]

While Cronbach's Alpha tends to provide a severe underestimation of the internal consistency reliability of latent variables in PLS path models, it is more appropriate to apply a different measure, the composite reliability [Werts et al., 1974].

The composite reliability takes into account that indicators have different loadings, and can be interpreted in the same way as Cronbach's Alpha. No matter which particular reliability coefficient is used, an internal consistency reliability value above 0.7 in early stages of research and values above 0.8 or 0.9 in more advanced stages of research are regarded as satisfactory, whereas a value below 0.6 indicates a lack of reliability.

Criterion	Model Type	Measuring Model quality metrics
Cronbach's Alpha	R	Cronbach's Alpha provides an estimate for the reliability based on the indicator intercorrelations. Values should be higher than 0.7.
Composite Reliability	R	The composite reliability is a measure of internal consistency and must not be lower than 0.6.
Average Variance extracted	R	AVE measures the amount of variance captured by the construct relative to the amount of variance due to measurement error. Values should be higher than 0.5.
Fornell-Larcker Criterion	R	For ensuring discriminant validity of latent variables, AVE should be higher than squared correlations with all other latent variables.
Cross Loadings	R	Cross loadings offer another possibility for checking discriminant validity. If an indicator has a higher correlation with another latent variable, the appropriateness of the model should be reconsidered.

Notes. R: reflective

Table 7.2.: Quality Metrics for the Measurement Model

Table 7.2 and Table 7.3 show further quality metrics and their description in the context of PLS-calculation of structural equation models.

7.3. Conclusion

In this chapter, a general methodology for using SEM in usability research was developed. Furthermore, a short discussion on SEM and connecting assumptions and calculation algorithms was presented. Additionally, one possibility of developing manifest variables for latent usability attributes was proposed.

Finally, extracted metrics for ensuring statistical quality of measurement and structural model were deduced.

A short discussion on SEM calculation algorithms is presented. It is confirmed that PLS gives reliable results if the following requirements are fulfilled:

- Phenomena explored are new without existing construct and measuring theories
- Structural model includes a large number of indicating variables
- Research design focuses on relative small sample size - Detection of causal paths and predictions is focused on

Criterion	Structural Model quality metrics
R2	Chin (1998) described R2 values of 0.67, 0.33 and 0.19 for endogenous latent variables as substantial, moderate or weak.
Estimates for path coefficients	The estimated path regression weights should be evaluated in terms of sign, magnitude and significance.
Effect size f2	f2 can be viewed as an indicator whether a latent variable has a weak, medium or large effect at a structural level.
Stone Geisser-Criterion Q2	Q2-value is based on the blindfolding procedure: $Q^2 = 1 - (\sum_D SSE_o)/(\sum_D SSO_o)$ Q2 values should greater than 0.0.

Table 7.3.: Quality Metrics for the Structural Model

PLS is a powerful method of analysis because of the minimal demands on measurement scales, sample size, and residual distributions. Although PLS can be used for theory confirmation, it can also be used to suggest where relationships might or might not exist and to suggest propositions for later testing.

As a result of this chapter the following method for conducting a PLS-analysis in usability research is proposed:

1. Theoretical deduction of Hypotheses based on causal relations
2. Definition of manifest variables for measuring latent constructs
3. Calculation of the PLS-Algorithm
4. Quality assessment of structural and measurement model results
5. Result interpretation

PLS is based on least squares estimation with the primary objective of maximizing the explanation of variance in a structural equation model's dependent constructs. Literature suggests that PLS is primarily intended for causal-predictive analysis in situations of high complexity but low theoretical information [Chin, 1998].

The PLS method does not require strong theory and can be used as a theory-building method [Gefen et al., 2000]. Considering this, it is concluded that this method is appropriate to calculating structural models in usability research due to incomplete theoretic background findings and missing unified empirical proved measurement scales by now. As a consequence, this chapter builds the basis for the following empirical analysis conducted in chapter 8.

8. Impact of Metaproperties on the Usability of Graphical Modeling Languages

In this chapter the impact of metamodel properties on usability attributes in the domain of graphical modeling languages is analyzed. The study is based on a model of hypotheses including two structural models depending on particular user scenario. The models were developed under consideration of psychological cognitive theories and usability theory. Survey data is collected and the causal relations hypotheses are assessed using a structure equation modeling approach. The outcome of this study shows important findings for practical and theoretical issues of how differing modeling languages are influencing usability attributes on causal stages in the modeling domain. The main focus of this chapter is to define differences and similarities of how language metaproperties impact on usability attributes in model development and model interpretation scenarios. This chapter aims to answer the research question Q2 "How do different modeling languages impact on different usability attributes" [Schalles et al., 2011b].

Considering the FUEML Framework, the usability concept in the domain of graphical modeling languages is specified by learnability, memorability, effectiveness, efficiency, and user satisfaction [Schalles et al., 2010a]. In case of model interpretation scenarios the attribute of visual perceptibility is introduced. The proposition is that these attributes and especially their causal interaction influence the usability of modeling languages.

Usability literature and transferred theories only set the different attributes on one causal level. For example, Nielsen (2006) and Abran et al. (2003) state that usability is affected by attributes with same weightings [Nielsen, 2006a, Abran et al., 2003]. The general idea behind this analysis is that the usability of modeling languages is defined by chosen attributes on different stages. Furthermore, a causal interaction between usability attributes, which is examined in this empirical research, is proposed.

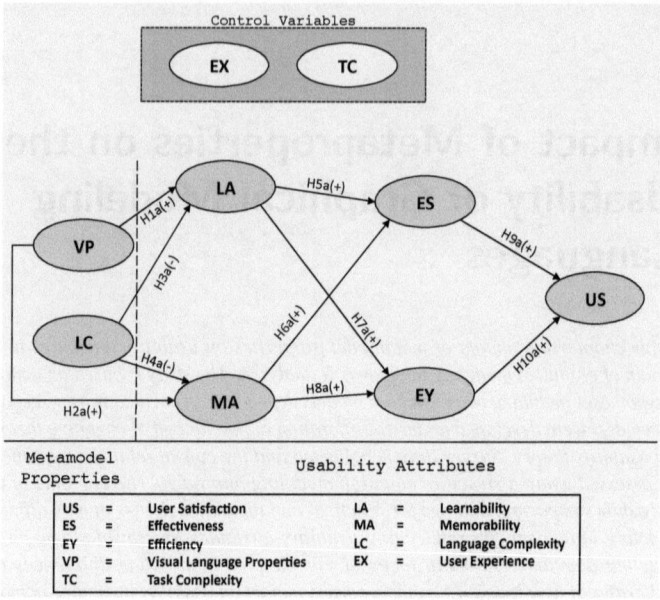

Figure 8.1.1.: Structural Model for Development Scenarios

8.1. Model Development Scenarios

The research model includes two basic parts, the metamodel properties and the attributes defining usability. Metamodel properties are set in language's metamodel. They are language specific attributes, which affect the usability attributes on different stages. Past research analyzed three antecedents, which impact the construction of knowledge extracted of models [Gemino and Wand, 2003, Oei et al., 1992]: Content, visual presentation and model viewer characteristics. The content represents the domain information to be communicated. The presentation method is the way content is presented, including semantics, syntax, colors, symbols, and media. Model viewer characteristics are attributes of the viewer prior to viewing the content.

For the general alignment of the usability attributes in this model a chronological order is assumed. For example, a user learns and memorizes the application of a modeling language. Consequently, this user is able to apply the modeling language and finally, this user may evaluate the modeling language.

Additionally, the actual language-based attributes, which transfer information, can be found in semantics, syntax, element colors and element shapes of specific modeling language [Burton et al., 2009]. Consequently, these variables are subsumed as exogenous variables, visual properties (VP) and language complexity (LC), in the structural model.

8.1.1. Hypotheses for Model Development Scenarios

The hypotheses supported by theory for model development scenarios (a) are presented in this section. The hypotheses supported by theory for model interpretation scenarios (b) are presented in subsection 8.2.1.

> *HYPOTHESIS 1a. The range of different element colors and geometrics set in the language's metamodel (VP) are positively influencing user's ability to learn the development of models by applying a particular modeling language (LA)*

With considering perceptive factors affecting modeling languages' usability visual based metrics such as the number of different element shapes and the number of different element colors were defined [Elsuwe and Schmedding, 2001]. Hall and Hanna (2004) analyzed the impact of color on web usability attributes in an empirical survey. They concluded that the application of different colors results in a higher grade of website structuredness, which leads to more efficient information processing in the user's brain [Hall and Hanna, 2004]. Due to the fact that today users apply computer systems for model developing models, it is concluded that these findings can be transferred to this survey. It is assumed that the variance of different geometric shapes depicting different element types is positively influencing the learnability of developing models by applying a specific language. The theoretic basis for this assumption is initially given by Comber and Maltby (1997). They concluded that screen structuredness including the application of various geometric shapes is a positive influencing variable of usability and especially learnability. However, they additionally underlay a positive trade-off between screen structuredness and learnability [Comber and Maltby, 1997]. It is stated that this hypothesis (H1a) is validated for model development scenarios.

> *HYPOTHESIS 2a. The range of different element colors and geometrics set in the language's metamodel (VP) are positively influencing user's ability to remember the elements and syntax of the modeling language (MA)*

Hall and Hanna (2004) analyzed a strong impact of visual properties on information structuredness [Hall and Hanna, 2004]. Furthermore, Nembhard and Napassavong (2002) found a positive correlation between structured information and information storage in human's brain [Nembhard and Napassavong, 2002]. Moody (2009) subsumes the visual element variability of graphical modeling languages in retinal variables including shapes and colors [Moody, 2009]. Deducing this to the structural model leads to the fact that the visual variability of modeling languages is positively influencing the user's ability to remember elements and syntax of modeling languages in model development tasks (H2a).

HYPOTHESIS 3a. The complexity of a modeling language (LC) affects negatively the probands' ability to learn this language (LA)

Referring to Rossi and Brinkkemper (1996) the sum of

- elements,
- relations
- and properties

can be abstracted and defined as modeling language complexity. The language complexity influences the usability attributes [Siau and Rossi, 2008]. For analyzing the language's complexity Welke (1992) and additionally Rossi and Brinkkemper (1996) developed metrics based on the OPRR data model [Welke, 1992, Rossi and Brinkkemper, 1996]. Transferring this, metrics such as the number of object types (i.e. class), number of relationship types (i.e. association) and the number of property types (i.e. class name) are relevant for analyzing the complexity of a modeling language. The more elements, relations and properties a modeling language consists of, the more difficult a user can learn the application due to high semantic and syntactic power. For model development scenarios a high Language Complexity causes that a user has to choose the semantic and syntactic correct elements and relations (H3a) established in the metamodel of the graphical modeling language.

HYPOTHESIS 4a. Language complexity (LC) affects negatively the user's ability to remember elements, relations and syntax within a period of non use/training (MA)

According to Kintsch (1998) cognitive processes underlie comprehension of a specific domain [Kintsch, 1998]. Nembhard and Napassavong (2002) found out that the complexity of a special domain influences memorability negatively [Nembhard and Napassavong, 2002]. According to the approach presented here, it is assumed that metamodel complexity is negatively related to memorability of modeling languages. A high semantically and syntactical complexity of language's metamodel is complicating language application due to hindered ability of remembering elements, relations and their specific application.

HYPOTHESIS 5a. The gradient of a language's learning curve (LA) is positively related to the ability of completing a task with minimal errors and maximal completeness (ES)

The ability of learning a modeling language in an easy or difficult way influences the language's effectiveness in model development (H5a) and model interpretation (H5b) when the language is applied. On the one hand it is implied that low learnability values of a modeling language result in rising error rates and decreasing task completion rates. On the other hand it is assumed that an easy to learn modeling language supports task completion rates and lowers error rates. In cognitive psychology low gradients of learning curves causes ineffective application of a construct in a specific domain [Anderson, 1985]. Therefore, the underlying assumption is that modeling languages, which are difficult to learn, offer a limited user individual application. This influences task completion rates and task error rates, which are manifest variables for measuring the latent construct effectiveness.

HYPOTHESIS 6a. The user's ability to remember the range of elements, relations and syntactic regulations (MA) is positively related to the user's ability of performing tasks with minimal errors and maximal completeness (ES)

Memorability describes the "remembering rate" of a modeling language. Overall it describes the fact that a modeling language should be easy to remember regarding its elements, syntax and semantics [Mayer, 1989]. Memorability is a very important attribute for measuring the usability of modeling languages considering that users may not be using a modeling language all the time [Nielsen, 2006a]. Hence, it is hypothesized that a modeling language, which is easy to remember results in less errors and higher completion rates in model development tasks.

HYPOTHESIS 7a. The gradient of a language's learning curve (LA) is positively related to the efficiency (EY) that is offered by modeling languages during applying them

Learnability is probably the most important attribute of usability, since a modeling language needs to be easy to learn. Learning to use a modeling language in development scenarios seems to be the first experience most users are confronted with a new modeling language [Siau and Rossi, 2008, Mayer, 1989]. Easy to learn languages offer a higher user-individual learning growth and consequently higher curve gradients based on task completion time values than difficult to learn modeling languages [Tamir et al., 2008]. It is stated that this effect supports efficiency in the modeling domain.

HYPOTHESIS 8a. The user's ability to remember the range of elements, relations and syntactic regulations (MA) is positively related to efficient task accomplishment (EY) offered by the modeling language

Usability research shows that memorability is an initial basis for applying a system or a website [Nielsen, 2006a]. Transferring this it is stated that some modeling languages are easier to remember than other. For example, it seems that BPMN elements are not easy to remember because of its high range of different element types. From this fact can be deduced that an efficient use and consequently a fast task completion is influenced by the memorability of the different metamodel properties a language consists of.

HYPOTHESIS 9a. The ability to perform a task with minimal errors and maximal completeness (ES) is positively related to user's individual satisfaction (US) with a modeling language

Effectiveness characterizes the fact, that it should be possible to reach a successful task accomplishment. In this regard, a user should be able to develop models with low error rates and high task completion rates [Bobkowska, 2005a, Wand and Weber, 1993]. Regarding the usability of modeling languages in the development scenario it can be deduced that languages offering

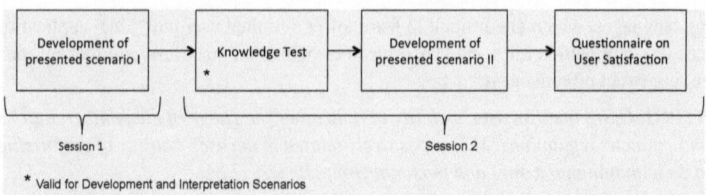

Figure 8.1.2.: Process of Data Collection for Model Development Scenarios

high effectiveness result in higher user satisfaction values. In contrast, it is stated that languages offering low effectiveness values affect user's individual satisfaction negatively.

> *HYPOTHESIS 10a. The Efficiency of task completion (EY) is positively related to user's individual satisfaction (US) of modeling languages*

A modeling language is efficient to use when users are able to develop or comprehend a model relatively quickly and correctly regarding the regulations of the modeling language. Once a user has learned a modeling language it should be possible to reach a high level productivity regarding task completion time [Bobkowska, 2005b, Wand and Weber, 1993]. Hence, it is hypothesized that languages, which afford an efficient task completion in model development scenarios (H10a), result in higher values concerning user satisfaction.

8.1.2. Research Methodology

8.1.2.1. Data Collection

The data collection was based on two different modeling concepts and connected languages. On the one hand process based languages, Event driven Process Chains (EPC), UML Activity Diagrams and on the other hand structure based modeling languages, UML Use Case and UML Class Diagrams. For measuring learnability a second measuring point was introduced.

For model development the Bflow*-toolbox[1] and ArgoUML[2] modeling tools were applied. At the beginning of second data collection phase the knowledge tests for measuring the ability of remembering specific metalevel properties were distributed. Subsequently, the User Satisfaction Questionnaire was administered to the participants.

---

[1] http://www.bflow.org
[2] http://www.argouml.tigris.org

8.1.2.2. Measurement Scales

In this section chosen manifest variables working as indicators for latent constructs in the research model are theoretically underlain. The general idea is transferred from the FUEML evaluation framework proposed in chapter 4. However, various adaptions to the structural models has been made and are introduced in the following paragraphs.

Effectiveness   Evaluating effectiveness requires analysis of task output with measuring quantity and quality of goal achievement [Rengger et al., 1993]. Quantity is defined as the proportion of task goals represented in the output of a task. Quality is the degree to which the task goals represented in the output have been achieved [Bevan and Macleod, 1994]. Bevan (1995) defined effectiveness as a product of quantity and quality [Bevan, 1995]. Transferring this to the proposed research model, indicating manifest variables for measuring effectiveness are the grade of completeness and the grade of correctness of model development tasks [Schalles et al., 2010a].

Efficiency   The efficiency is the amount of human, economical and temporal resources. Measures of efficiency relate to the level of effectiveness achieved to the expenditure of resources [Bevan and Macleod, 1994]. Measure values of efficiency include time taken to complete tasks, i.e. duration time for performing model development tasks [Vuolle et al., 2008].

1. Model Development Time in seconds

Learnability   Learnability describes the ease of learning the application of modeling languages in model development scenarios. For this characteristic, the standard measure values are based on task completion rates and the task accuracy [Seffah et al., 2006]. In general, learnability is a development and can be graphically described by learning curves [Tamir et al., 2008]. Hence, learnability can be measured by the rate of difference when the user repeats evaluation sessions [Bevan, 1995]. Nielsen (2006) insists that highly learnable systems could be categorized as "allowing users to reach a reasonable level of usage proficiency (...)" [Nielsen, 2006a]. Furthermore, Nielsen (2006) proposes measuring proficiency by quantity and quality and of task fulfillment. Thus, grade of completeness and grade of correctness were chosen as basic variables for measuring learnability. With conducting two measuring points mp and $mp + 1$, it is possible to analyze the relative difference for indicating Δ learnability, i.e. individual learning progress in percent [Nembhard and Napassavong, 2002, Grossman et al., 2009].

The applied variables for measuring learnability in this survey are calculated as follows:

1. $Grade\,of\,completeness_{mp+1} - Grade\,of\,completeness_{mp}$
2. $Grade\,of\,correctness_{mp+1} - Grade\,of\,correctness_{mp}$

Memorability   Memorability is best measured as proficiency after a period of non-use provided a user has already learned a language [Olle et al., 1986]. The non-use period can be minutes for simple element meanings, hours for simple syntactic regulations and days or weeks for measuring a complete modeling language [Seffah et al., 2006]. Accordingly, the measure values for memorability are neglect curves and time-delayed knowledge tests [Nembhard and Uzumeri, 2000]. Concerning the usability of modeling languages, the user must remember the different elements and its intended meaning (semantics), the syntax and the application. In due consideration of Nielsen (2006), the measuring points interval should be several weeks regarding memorability [Nielsen, 2006a]. Thus, for measuring memorability it was decided to use a knowledge test consisting of items focusing on

1. elements and relations,

2. syntax and

3. application of particular language.

User Satisfaction   Compared to the other latent variables in our research model, the individual satisfaction of a user while developing or interpreting a model is a user subjective criterion that can be measured best by using standardized questionnaires [Vuolle et al., 2008]. Currently no standardized method for measuring user satisfaction in the modeling domain exists. Therefore, questionnaires focusing on system and website usability were mapped [Kirakowski and Corbett, 1993, Armstrong et al., 2005]. For evaluating user satisfaction a questionnaire was developed, which consists of thirty items structured in

1. general impression,

2. recommendation rate and

3. language application.

The constructs were measured with 5-point Likert-scales. The development of this questionnaire is generally contributing to the Questionnaire for User Interaction Satisfaction (QUIS) and additionally the Software Usability Measurement Inventory (SUMI) [Chin and Lee, 2000, Kirakowski and Corbett, 1993]. In addition to that, variables focusing on user perception for measuring user satisfaction in the research model were specified [Maes and Poels, 2007].

Language Complexity   The exogenous variable language complexity was tracked track by number of different elements, number of different relations and number of different properties (LC) under consideration of Rossi and Brinkkemper's (1996) OPRR-model and particular expansions by Recker et al. (2009) and Indulska et al. (2009) [Rossi and Brinkkemper, 1996, Recker and Dreiling, 2007, Indulska et al., 2009]. A detailed deduction of those properties is given in the FUEML framework in chapter 2.

1. number of elements

2. number of relations

3. number of properties

Visual Properties   Furthermore, for indicating visual properties findings of Bertin (1983) and Moody and Heymans (2010)were adopted. Hence, there are six retinal visual variables, which can be used to graphically encode information: Shape, Size, Color, Brightness, Orientation and Texture. Those variables are structured in color (color, brightness, texture) and shapes (shape, size, orientation), which are defined in a language's metamodel [Bertin, 1983] [Moody and Heymans, 2010].

Consequently, the number of different colors and the number of different geometric shapes act as variables for measuring visual properties (VP).

1. number of different shapes

2. number of different colors

Moderators   Additionally, two moderating variables, which affect causal relations in our model were analyzed. First, the participant's experience of developing or interpreting models and secondly the particular complexities of development or interpretation tasks influence the causal relations in our study. For measuring modeling experience, participant's individual experiences in

1. general modeling experience and

2. language experience on a 5-point Likert-scale are tracked.

Finally, model complexity is operationalized by three indicator variables:

1. number of elements and relations (size),

2. connectivity degree

3. semantic spread.

Table 8.1 provides an overview of applied items for measuring the latent constructs:

8.1.2.3. Pretest

A pretest was conducted prior collecting data for the field test. The research instruments were tested for reliability, content validity and construct validity. Necessary changes were made to improve measuring instruments. All pilot test participants were excluded from the analysis sample.

Constructs	Measurement Items
Visual Properties (VP)	Number of different colors
	Number of different shapes
Language Complexity (LC)	Number of elements
	Number of relations
	Number of properties
Learnability (LA)	Δ Grade of Correctness
	Δ Grade of Completeness
Memorability (MA)	Elements and relations
	Syntax
	Application
Effectiveness (ES)	Grade of completeness of model development
	Grade of correctness of model development
Efficiency (EY)	Model development time in s
User Satisfaction (US)	I am likely to choose this language for modeling my business cases
	I recommend this language without any concerns
	The application of this language is circumstantial
	The application of this language is frustrating
	My expectations for that language are fulfilled
	Developing a model by applying this language was easy
	Developing a model by applying this language was successful
	I was able to develop the given scenario completely
	I was able to develop the given scenario accurately
	The number of different elements and relations in language's metamodel are confusing
	It was difficult to remember language's elements
	Remembering language's syntax was difficult
	Visual analogue Scale
Task (Model) Complexity (TC)	Size
	Connectivity Degree
	Semantic Spread
User Experience (EX)	Language Experience
	Modeling Experience

Table 8.1.: Measurement Items for Model Development Scenarios

8.1.3. Data Analysis and Results

To test the proposed research model, data analyses for both the measurement model and the structural model were performed using PLS, bootstrapping and the blindfolding method [Tenenhaus et al., 2005]. For the calculation SmartPLS version 2.0 M3 was chosen[3]. Chin et al. (2003) defined various strengths of the PLS-approach [Chin et al., 2003]. Although PLS can be used for theory confirmation, it can also be used to suggest where relationships might or might not exist and to suggest propositions for later testing [Chin, 1998].

8.1.3.1. Validity and Reliability

An exploratory factor analysis in SPSS 19 for each construct of the model was conducted including all defined items using an oblique rotation (Promax). Compared to orthogonal rotation methods, Promax assumes that the factors are correlated. Fabrigar et al. (1999) concluded that human behavior is rarely partitioned into neatly packaged units that function independently of one another [Fabrigar et al., 1999]. Hence, some correlation among factors is expected.

In all cases the Bartlett-test of sphericity indicating independency of construct items among was accepted. Consequently, different factors were analyzed and variables were assigned to specific factors considering Kaiser's criterion [Kaiser, 1974]. Indicating acceptable validity, items with loadings smaller than 0.5 should be excluded from the research model. However, in our case, all item loadings exceed the threshold of 0.5. Consequently, no items were excluded. A detailed presentation of these values is given in the appendix A.3. (pnline supplement)

Multiple indicators measured all but one construct. The exception was EY, which represents a discrete value and therefore can be appropriately measured with a single item focusing on task completion time. Language Complexity (LC), Memorability (MA), Learnability (LA), Effectiveness (ES) and User Experience (EX) were conceptualized and measured as aggregations of different manifestations; thus the direction of causality is from indicator to construct (i.e. formative). The other constructs were operationalized as reflective indicators.

8.1.3.2. Missing Data

As the research instrument of this study contains several collection methods such as questionnaire, knowloedge test and empirical tasks the possibility of missing data was deemed reasonable. The rate of missing values in the dataset is less than two percent. For dealing with missing values the multiple imputation method offered by SPSS 19 was chosen.

Multiple imputation accounts for missing data by restoring not only the natural variability in the data, but also by incorporating the incertainty caused by estimating missing data. The

---

[3]SmartPLS is a software application for the modeling of Structural Equation Models (SEM) and their calculation with the methodology of the Partial Least Squares (PLS) approach [Ringle et al., 2011].

performance of multiple imputation in a variety of missing data situations has been well-studied and it has been shown to perform favorably in connection with PLS [Lynn, 2006].

8.1.3.3. Testing the Measurement Model

Internal consistency reliability for our model was evaluated using Cronbach's Alpha, corrected item total correlation and average variance extracted (AVE) [Fornell and Larcker, 1981]. Cronbach's Alpha coefficients were all higher than the proposed minimum cutoff score of 0.70 [Nunnally and Bernstein, 1994]. Alpha values for Experience (EX) are marginally less (i.e.0.68) than minimum threshold. However, [Barker et al., 1994] conclude that values between 0.60 and 0.70 are marginal. Furthermore, all reflective constructs had an minimum AVE of 0.5, indicating adequate internal consistency of our model [74].

For testing reliability of formative constructs, R2-value proposed by Chin (1998) with a minimum cutoff of 0.3 was analyzed [Chin, 1998]. Furthermore, Diamantopoulos and Winklhofer (2001) concluded that sufficient significant regression weights between formative constructs and other constructs in the path model are indicating formal construct validity [Diamantopoulos and Winklhofer, 2001].

As shown in the following section all relevant path regression weights are at least significant at 0.05-level. According to Fornell and Larcker (1981), constructs have adequate discriminant validity if the square root of AVE is higher than variance shared between construct and other constructs in the model [Fornell and Larcker, 1981]. In all cases the correlations between each pair of constructs were lower than the square root of the AVE for specific construct. In conclusion, these results confirm that all constructs in our model are empirically distinct.

Table 8.2 shows the applied quality metrics for ensuring reliability of the SEM.

8.1.3.4. Testing the Structural Model

Figure 8.1.3 and Figure 8.2.3 present the results of structural model testing including regression weights and significance of the paths. According to Lohmöller (1989), path regression weights should be at least 0.10 in order to be considered meaningful for discussion [Lohmöller, 1989].

Our results confirmed the general assumption that language's metamodel properties are influencing usability attributes on different stages. According to Chin (1998) and for ensuring complete model assessment, effect size f2, which is indicating whether a path's latent exogenous variable has a significant influence (effect) on latent endogenous variable or not is shown additionally. Thresholds for f2 are 0.02 (weak), 0.15 (medium) and 0.35 (strong) [Chin, 1998].

LC has a strong negative and highly significant impact on MA (beta=-0.934, f2=0.59, p<0.001). This result supports hypothesis H4a. Against the theoretic based expectation the influence of LC on LA is neither strong nor significant (beta=-0.038, f2=0.01). Furthermore, VP is strongly

		Measurement Model		Structural Model		
	Type	Alpha	Composite Reliability	AVE	R^2	Q^2
Threshold		≥ 0.7	≥ 0.7	≥ 0.5	≥ 0.19	≥ 0.0
VP	R	0.97	0.98	0.97	NA+	0.83
LC	F	NA	NA	NA	NA+	0.39
MA	F	NA	NA	NA	0.49	0.24
LA	F	NA	NA	NA	0.34	0.13
EY	R	1.00	1.00	1.00	0.26	0.26
ES	F	NA	NA	NA	0.44	0.29
US	R	0.87	0.88	0.54	0.20	0.12
TC	R	0.96	0.97	0.93	NA+	0.79
EX	R	0.68	0.52	0.72	NA+	0.71

Notes. R: reflective, F: formative; n=114 for all constructs; NA: not applicable: because formative measures need not covary, the internal consistency of formative items is not applicable [Chin, 1998]. NA+: not applicable: because R2 value is only relevant for assessing endogenous latent variables in the inner structural model [Chin, 1998].

Table 8.2.: Model Quality for Development Scenarios

Constructs	ES	EX	EY	LA	LC	MA	TC	US	VP
ES	**NA**								
EX	0.21	**0.85**							
EY	0.21	-0.76	**1.00**						
LA	*0.02*	0.31	*0.42*	**NA**					
LC	0.14	0.17	0.06	*-0.04*	**NA**				
MA	0.29	0.23	*0.05*	0.05	-0.93	**NA**			
TC	-0.52	0.30	-0.34	0.27	0.23	0.06	**0.96**		
US	*0.46*	0.13	-0.12	0.24	0.27	0.34	-0.42	**0.59**	
VP	0.17	0.59	0.25	*0.82*	0.60	*-0.05*	0.53	0.40	**0.99**

Notes. (1) Diagonal elements are the square root of average variance extracted (AVE). These values should exceed the interconstruct correlations for adequate discriminant validity. (2) The italic values show correlations included in our structural models. (3) NA - Does not apply for formative measures.

Table 8.3.: Latent Variable Correlations for Development Scenarios

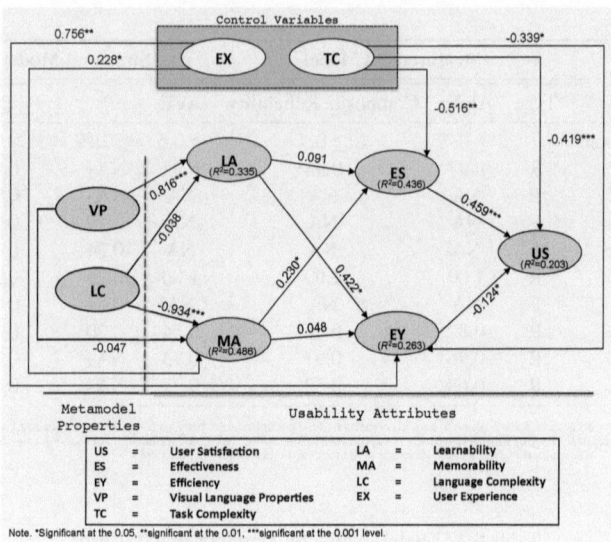

Figure 8.1.3.: Results for Development Scenarios

connected to LA, which is contributing to H1a (beta=0.816, f2=0.23, p<0.001). Contrariwise, the impact of VP on MA is not significant (beta=-0.047, f2=0.029). Consequently, H2a is rejected.

MA is positively influencing ES, which is contributing to H6a (beta=0.230, f2=0.21, p<0.01). However, MA is not significantly influencing EY and consequently H8a is not supported by the results (beta=0.048, f2=0.01). LA is positively impacting on EY (beta=0.422, f2=0.14, p<0.05). This result is supporting H7a. Furthermore, the results show that H5a, which is defining causal path between LA and ES, is not supported (beta=0.091, f2=0.16). Additionally, a strong positive correlation between ES and US (beta=0.459, f2=0.28, p<0.001) exists. This result is supporting H9a. Finally, the results explain a negative correlation between EY and US (beta=-0.124, f2=0.17, p<0.05). This fact is not contributing to H10a.

Turning to model fit, the R-square values for MA, LA, EY, ES and US were 0.486, 0.335, 0.263, 0.436, and 0.203, indicating that the model explains substantial variation in these variables. For example, the R-square value for MA implies that the causes specified in this model, VP and LC, jointly explain 49% of the total variance in MA. In summary, the results show that most hypotheses in the research model for model development scenario are fully supported.

However, H10a is not supported by the results. Furthermore, H2a, H3a, H5a and H8a could not be confirmed by significant results. As a consequence, particular hypotheses are not confirmed

No.	Path
1	$VP \rightarrow LA \rightarrow EY \rightarrow US$
2	$VP \rightarrow MA \rightarrow ES \rightarrow US$

Table 8.4.: Causal Paths in Development Scenarios

for further comparable samples. The resulting regression weights are valid for the specific sample and should be proved in further surveys based on this research model.

8.1.4. Analyzing Causal Paths in the Research Model

The results underline the assumption that the usability attributes are influenced by various metamodel properties on different stages. Different causal paths influencing usability attributes dependent on particular scenario and triggered by metamodel properties (i.e. LC vs. VP) were analyzed in the structural model. Although various scientific discussions on the term of causality do exist, the relation of cause and effect can be emphasized as generally accepted criterion of causality.

Under consideration of Blalock (1982) as well as Cook and Campell (1979) the term of assumed causal path for the following section is introduced [Blalock, 1982, Cook and Campell, 1979]. As Cook and Campell (1979) concluded, a causal relation between independent and dependent variables exist on the following terms:

1. Variations of the independent variable result in variations of the dependent variable

2. A chronological sequence does exist

3. Independent variable is the sole impact factor if the dependent variable

Table 8.4 shows assumed causal relations and marked significant paths in interpretation scenarios based on the empirical results. The findings described in this section underline the general hypothesis that Visual Properties and Language Complexity both set in language's metamodel act as exogenous latent variables in the research model.

Causal Path 1 The use of multiple colors and geometric shapes (VP) in language's metamodel supports LA and EY positively in model development scenarios. The theoretical reason is that various colors and shapes lead to more information structuredness [Hall and Hanna, 2004]. We deduce that the grade of structuredness of information has positive effects on learnability and consequently the efficiency [Sweller, 2005]. From this result we deduce, that languages including various element shapes and colors in the metamodel are easier to learn regarding developing models than languages offering less shape and color variation. Consequently, we conclude that for example learning developing models with EPC's is easier than with UML-Activity-Diagrams or BPMN. Furthermore we reason that VP impacts on EY indirectly. From this follows, that languages including various element shapes and colors in the metamodel support a fast task accomplishment in development scenarios. We found out that time used for task completion in model development scenarios is not positively impacting on User Satisfaction. This might be underlining former findings of Walker (1998). In their studies they found out that users have demonstrated preferences for systems with which they performed less efficiently [Walker et al., 1998].

Causal Path 2   Form the results is derived that the number of elements, relations and properties (LC) is negatively influencing memorability in development tasks. For finding a theoretical background for this result we start with applying Sweller's Cognitive Load Theory [Sweller, 2005]. They analyzed three loads, which are defining human working memory during instruction. Human's working memory is a basis for extracting, processing and storing information. In our case we focus on intrinsic cognitive load. Intrinsic cognitive load is influenced by information complexity. Transferring this to our research we conclude that LC impacts user's intrinsic cognitive load. Sweller (2005) proposes reducing information complexity to keep intrinsic cognitive load low. With considering this we come to the conclusion that complex modeling languages such as BPMN are offering worse memorability than less complex languages such as UML-activity-diagrams. Additionally, MA is positively supporting ES and consequently US. From this we conclude that ability to complete model development tasks completely and correctly is highly correlating to User Satisfaction values. In conclusion, modeling languages offering low metamodel complexity i.e. EPC's, UML-Use-Case-diagrams, support user's individual satisfaction with developing a model based on particular language.

8.1.5. Total Effects of Metaproperties

The causal effects appearing between the latent constructs in our research model, can be separated into direct, indirect and total effects. A general causal effect between two variables X and Y can be formally defined as follows: $P(y/do(x))$ [Pearl, 2000]. For example, from this is deduced that the causal relation between LC and MA can be described as $P(MA/do(LC))$. A total causal effect is defined as the sum of direct and indirect effects transmitted through intermediate variables. After calculating the total effects of usability impacting metaproperties of modeling languages, it is possible to analyze the total impact of variations of LC and VP on each usability attribute. For each usability attribute the standardized total effects of LC and VP are shown in figure 3:

First, this analysis shows that the complexity of language's metamodel influences all defined usability attributes in development scenarios negatively. In general, this means that the relation between language complexity and the defined usability attributes is inverse (except effectiveness). As a consequence, increasing language complexity by e.g. adding elements and relations

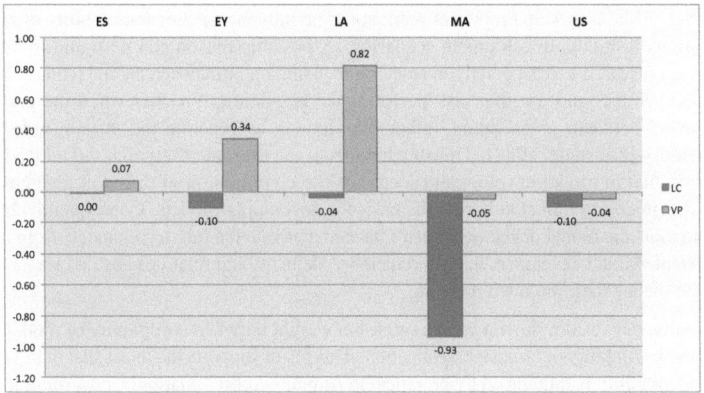

Figure 8.1.4.: Total Effects in Development Scenarios

influences all defined usability attributes in development scenarios negatively. Concerning this, memorability is influenced most by complexity rise (-0.93).

Another interesting finding is that an effective task accomplishment (ES) is not caused by language complexity (-0.00) in development scenarios. Furthermore, the total effect of language complexity on learnability is comparable low (-0.04).

Second, for visual properties (VP), the total effect on the defined usability attributes is in all cases positive. It becomes obvious that the total effect variance of VP between usability attributes is not as high as LC.

8.1.6. Discussion for Model Development Scenarios

The results show that the complexity of particular modeling language is strongly negatively influencing user's ability of remembering elements and relations. Traditional usability research shows that memorability is an initial basis for efficient website or system application [Nielsen, 2006b]. With the structural model results, those theses for model development scenarios cannot be confirmed.

Memorability is weakly influencing efficiency. The ability of remembering elements and relations is positively influencing user's ability of accurate and complete performance of model development tasks. However, it seems that memorability plays an important role in model development scenarios. Furthermore, our results show that visual language properties are primarily strongly impacting learnability of language application.

In contrast, visual language properties seem not to be influencing the memorability of elements and relations in model development scenarios. A possible reason can be found in cognitive information research and especially in research focusing on human screen and icon recognition. Lansdale (1988) found out that task performance is essentially easier when the participant has to select between given items, rather than having to generate the missing information from memory [Lansdale, 1988]. Transferring this to the presented research model leads to the conclusion that in model development scenarios the combination of different given elements (e.g. in the modeling tool side-bar) is the basis for developing models. Consequently, by using modeling tools the model developer doesn't have to generate the missing elements from memory to full extent. Model developers have to remember elements and relations abstract semantics and as a consequence their intended meaning.

Additionally, our results show a weak regression weight between complexity of modeling languages and learnability of language application. This result supports the thesis that in information science learnability is influenced by graphical information representation. Concerning learnability, information complexity plays a secondary role in model development scenarios. Furthermore, the learnability of language application is strongly influencing efficiency in task performance. In contrast to that, learnability is not influencing effectiveness significantly. Finally, effectiveness, i.e. accurate and complete task performance is highly impacting on user satisfaction. On the other hand, efficiency is influencing user satisfaction negatively. This might be underlining former findings of Walker (1998). In their studies they found out that users have demonstrated preferences for systems with which they performed less efficiently [Walker et al., 1998].

8.2. Model Interpretation Scenarios

8.2.1. Hypotheses for Model Interpretation Scenarios

For the general alignment of the usability attributes in this model a chronological order is assumed. For example, a user learns and memorizes the application of a modeling language. Consequently, this user is able to apply the modeling language and finally, this user may evaluate the modeling language.

The causal hypotheses for model interpretation scenarios H1b - H10b are generally based on comparable hypotheses H1a - H10a of model development scenarios (see subsection 8.1.1).

> *HYPOTHESIS 1b. The range of different element colors and geometrics set in the language's metamodel (VP) are positively influencing user's ability to learn the interpretation of models (LA)*

> *HYPOTHESIS 2b. The range of different element colors and geometrics set in the language's metamodel (VP) are positively influencing user's ability to remember*

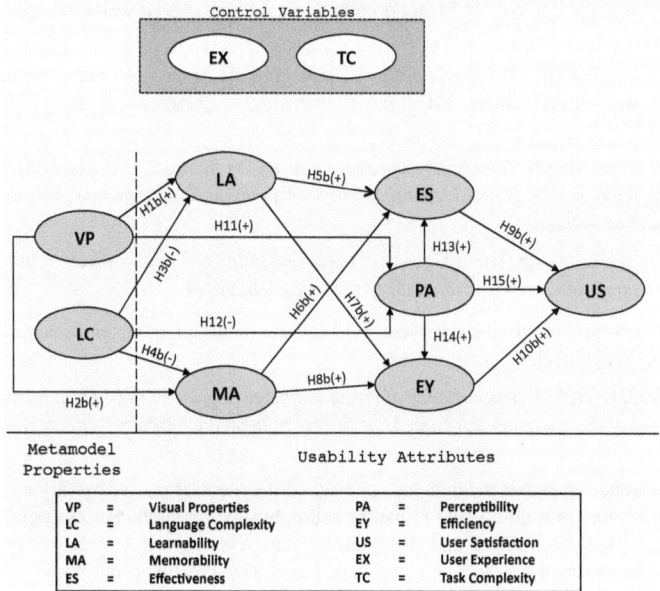

Figure 8.2.1.: Structural Model for Model Interpretation Scenarios

the elements and syntax of the modeling language in model interpretation scenarios (MA)

HYPOTHESIS 3b. The complexity of a modeling language (LC) affects negatively the probands' ability to learn this language in model interpretation scenarios (LA)

HYPOTHESIS 4b. Language complexity (LC) affects negatively the user's ability to remember elements, relations and syntax within a period of non use/training (MA)

HYPOTHESIS 5b. The gradient of a language's learning curve (LA) is positively related to the ability of completing a task with minimal errors and maximal completeness (ES)

HYPOTHESIS 6b. The user's ability to remember the range of elements, relations and syntactic regulations (MA) is positively related to the user's ability of performing tasks with minimal errors and maximal completeness (ES)

HYPOTHESIS 7b. The gradient of a language's learning curve (LA) is positively related to the efficiency (EY) that is offered by modeling languages during applying them

HYPOTHESIS 8b. The user's ability to remember the range of elements, relations and syntactic regulations (MA) is positively related to efficient model interpretation (EY)

HYPOTHESIS 9b. The ability to perform a task with minimal errors and maximal completeness (ES) is positively related to user's individual satisfaction (US) with a modeling language

HYPOTHESIS 10b. The Efficiency of task completion (EY) is positively related to user's individual satisfaction (US) of modeling languages

In the following section specific hypotheses H11-H15 for model interpretation scenarios including the method of eye-tracking are proposed:

HYPOTHESIS 11. The variance of visual language properties (VP) set in the meta-model of the modeling language is positively influencing language's perceptibility (PA)

Many researchers analyzed the influence of visual differentiation caused by varying geometric shapes and colors in usability and primarily neurophysical research. For example, Westphal and Würtz (2009) investigated that visual differentiation is supporting object recognition and consequently information search and information extraction [Westphal and Würtz, 2009]. However, in the structural model language's perceptibility is measured by values indicating cognitive processes e.g. information search and information extraction [Underwood, 2005]. Furthermore, Underwood (2009) corroborates the hypothesis that visual characteristics of an image are influencing eye movements [Underwood, 2009]. From this it is deduced, that visual language properties, i.e. colors, geometric shapes, are positively influencing language's perceptibility due to stronger visual differentiation in model diagrams.

HYPOTHESIS 12. The complexity of modeling languages (LC) is negatively influencing visual perceptibility (PA)

The complexity of modeling languages, which is set in the language's metamodel, is strongly connected with syntactical and semantical complexity. For example, UML Class Diagrams contain a high range of syntactically different relations (e.g. association, aggregation etc.), which can be expanded by cardinalities. Furthermore, a UML Class Diagram generally includes two different class types: standard and abstract classes. Pan et al. (2004) analyzed the viewing behavior of web pages by using an eye-tracker [Pan et al., 2004]. They come to the conclusion that visual complexity negatively contributes to eye-movement behavior due to difficulty of information search and information extraction. The resulting hypothesis is that syntactic and semantic language properties are negatively influencing the perceptibility of a diagram developed by the application of specific modeling languages.

HYPOTHESIS 13. The visual perceptibility (PA) of modeling languages is positively contributing to effective model interpretation (ES)

The objective of analyzing visual perceptibility is to measure processes of information search, information extraction and information processing in user's brain during model interpretation. For example, a low visual perceptibility of a model results in difficult information search and information extraction. Consequently, this fact is especially influencing task completion rate and subsequently effectiveness of model interpretation. Finally, it is hypothesized that visual perceptibility is influencing user's ability of ending an interpretation task with minimal errors and maximal completeness.

HYPOTHESIS 14. The visual perceptibility of modeling languages (PA) is positively contributing to efficient model interpretation (EY)

Goldberg and Kotval (1999) concluded that the number of overall fixations is negatively correlating with search efficiency. It is stated that this effect is influencing interpretation time and consequently interpretation efficiency [Goldberg and Kotval, 1999]. Furthermore, high fixation durations implicate participant's difficulty of extracting information from a model [Fitts et al., 1950]. Accordingly, this effect leads to increasing interpretation times and consequently lower efficiency.

HYPOTHESIS 15. The visual perceptibility (PA) of models developed by the application of modeling languages affects positively the user's satisfaction (US) of specific modeling languages

Many researchers concluded a strong impact of design (screen, website etc.) and especially layout and order of elements on target individual's satisfaction
[Sonderegger and Sauer, 2009, De Angeli et al., 2006]. Lindgaard (2007) states a positive link between user satisfaction and visual screen design [Lindgaard, 2007]. Subsequently, it is assumed that a high language's visual perceptibility results in higher user satisfaction.

8.2.2. Research Methodology

8.2.2.1. Data Collection

The data collection was based on two different modeling concepts and connected languages. On the one hand process based languages, Event driven Process Chains (EPC), UML Activity Diagrams and on the other hand structure based modeling languages, UML Use Case and UML Class Diagrams. In the model interpretation scenario the participants were confronted with several models developed by using the defined languages. Hereby, each interpretation process per session consists of two parts. In the first part participants were asked to gaze the presented model generally. During this period the basic values for eye tracking, fixation duration and the number of fixations, were collected. After that, participants were asked to analyze the entire

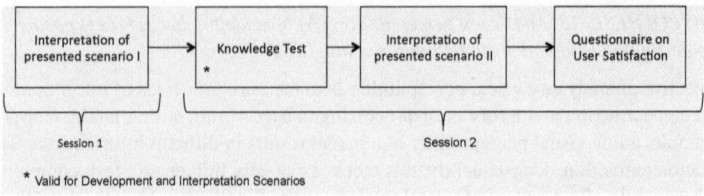

Figure 8.2.2.: Process of Data Collection for Model Interpretation Scenarios

model verbally. During the whole data collection phase the specific models were presented to the participants on screen.

8.2.2.2. Measurement Scales

The following table shows the items used for measuring the variables in model interpretation scenarios:

8.2.3. Data Analysis and Results

This section provides validity and reliability values of the structural model as well as the measurement model. Furthermore it shows the regression weights between the hypothesized causal paths. To test the proposed research model, data analyses for both the measurement model and the structural model were performed using PLS, bootstrapping and the blindfolding method [Tenenhaus et al., 2005]. For the calculation SmartPLS version 2.0 M3 was chosen[4].

8.2.3.1. Validity and Reliability

Similar to the development scenario, an exploratory factor analysis in SPSS for each construct of our models including all defined items using an oblique rotation (Promax) was conducted. In all cases the Bartlett-test of sphericity indicating independency of construct items among was accepted. Consequently, different factors were analyzed and variables were assigned to specific factors considering Kaiser's criterion [Kaiser, 1974]. Indicating acceptable validity, items with loadings smaller than 0.5 should be excluded from the research model. However, in the interpretation scenario, all item loadings exceed the threshold of 0.5. Consequently, no items were excluded. A detailed presentation of these values is given in the appendix A.3. (online supplement).

---

[4]SmartPLS is a software application for the modeling of Structural Equation Models (SEM) and their calculation with the methodology of the Partial Least Squares (PLS) approach [Ringle et al., 2011].

Constructs	Measurement Items
Visual Properties (VP)	Number of different colors
	Number of different shapes
Language Complexity (LC)	Number of elements
	Number of relations
	Number of properties
Learnability (LA)	Δ Grade of correct interpretation
	Δ Grade of complete interpretation
Memorability (MA)	Elements and relations
	Syntax
	Application
Effectiveness (ES)	Grade of correct interpretation
	Grade of complete interpretation
Efficiency (EY)	Model interpretation time in s
Perceptibility (PA)	Number of fixations
	Fixation length
User Satisfaction (US)	I am likely to choose this language for interpreting my business cases
	I recommend this language without any concerns
	The application of this language is circumstantial
	The application of this language is frustrating
	My expectations for that language are fulfilled
	Interpretation of given model was easy
	Comprehending the meaning of given model was successful
	Comprehending the meaning of given model was complete
	Comprehending the meaning of given model was fast
	The number of different elements and relations in language's metamodel are confusing
	Remembering different elements during model interpretation was difficult
	Remembering language's syntax during model interpretation was difficult
	Visual analogue Scale
Task (Model) Complexity (TC)	Size of interpreted model
	Connectivity Degree of interpreted model
	Semantic Spread of interpreted model
User Experience (EX)	Language Experience
	Modeling Experience

Table 8.5.: Measurement Items for Model Interpretation Scenarios

		Measurement Model		Structural Model		
	Type	Alpha	Composite Reliability	AVE	R^2	Q^2
Threshold		≥ 0.7	≥ 0.7	≥ 0.5	≥ 0.19	≥ 0.0
VP	R	0.96	0.98	0.97	NA+	0.78
LC	F	NA	NA	NA	NA+	0.58
MA	F	NA	NA	NA	0.47	0.24
LA	F	NA	NA	NA	0.20	0.10
EY	R	0.72	0.75	0.60	0.19	0.08
ES	F	NA	NA	NA	0.42	0.16
US	R	0.89	0.90	0.68	0.19	0.07
PA	R	0.78	0.88	0.88	0.20	0.09
TC	R	0.70	0.83	0.63	NA+	0.31
EX	R	0.68	0.62	0.52	NA+	0.66

Notes. R: reflective, F: formative; n=114 for all constructs; NA: not applicable: because formative measures need not covary, the internal consistency of formative items is not applicable [Chin, 1998]. NA+: not applicable: because R2 value is only relevant for assessing endogenous latent variables in the inner structural model [Chin, 1998].

Table 8.6.: Model Quality for Interpretation Scenarios

8.2.3.2. Missing Data

As the research instrument of this study contains several collection methods such as questionnaire, knowloedge test and empirical tasks the possibility of missing data was deemed reasonable. The rate of missing values in the dataset is less than two percent. For dealing with missing values the multiple imputation method offered by SPSS 19 was chosen.

Multiple imputation accounts for missing data by restoring not only the natural variability in the data, but also by incorporating the incertainty caused by estimating missing data. The performance of multiple imputation in a variety of missing data situations has been well-studied and it has been shown to perform favorably in connection with PLS [Lynn, 2006].

8.2.3.3. Testing the Measurement Model

Referring to the quality metrics deduced in subsubsection 8.1.3.3 it becomes obvious that the measurement model as well as the structural model are empirically distinct. Consequently, Cronbach's Alpha, Composite Reliability, Average Variance Extracted, Stone-Geisser-criterion Q^2 and R^2 fulfil the minimum cutoff proposed in literature.

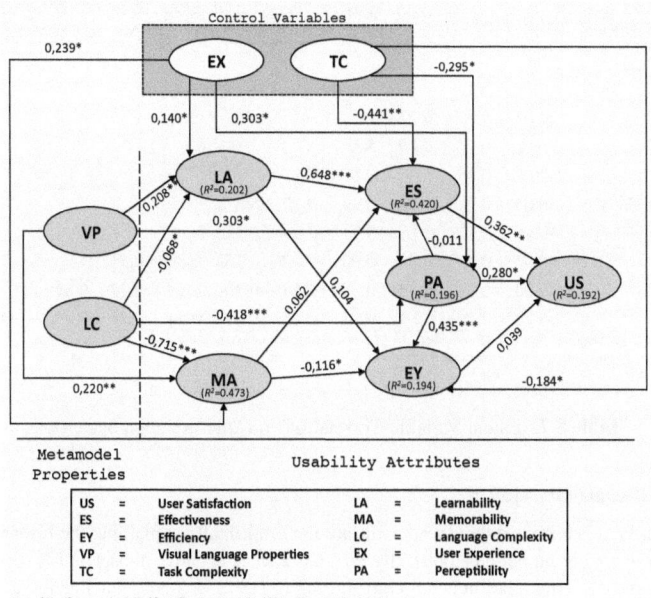

Figure 8.2.3.: Results for Interpretation Scenarios

8.2.3.4. Testing the Structural Model

LC has a strong negative and highly significant influence on MA (beta=-0.715, f2=0.80, p<0.001). This empirical result supports the hypothesis H4b. LC has also a strong significant negative impact on PA underlining H12b (beta=-0.418, f2=0.16, p<0.001). Furthermore, LC has a negative significant relation to LA contributing to H3b (beta=-0.068, f2=0.02, p<0.05). However, this path disposes not to Lohmöller's (1989) proposed threshold for path weighting of 0.1.

VP is positively influencing LA of applied modeling languages (beta=0.208, f2=0.02, p<0.01). In addition to that, VP is positively influencing PA (beta=0.303, f2=0.03, p<0.05). Considering this, all hypotheses in the research model connected with VP are accepted.

Additionally, LA is strongly positively related to ES on a high significance level (beta=0.648, f2=0.72, p<0.001), which is contributing to H5b. Furthermore, LA is positively affecting time based latent construct EY and MA is positively correlating with ES. These path regression weights are not significant (p>0.05). Deducing from that, the null hypothesis with probability

Constructs	ES	EX	EY	LA	LC	MA	TC	PA	US	VP
ES	**NA**									
EX	-0.11	**NA**								
EY	0.05	0.02	**0.77**							
LA	*0.65*	0.14	*0.10*	**NA**						
LC	-0.01	-0.45	0.00	*-0.07*	**NA**					
MA	*0.06*	0.24	*-0.12*	0.03	*-0.72*	**NA**				
TC	-0.44	0.17	-0.18	-0.21	-0.35	0.17	**0.79**			
PA	*-0.01*	0.30	*0.44*	0.03	*-0.42*	0.26	-0.30	**0.94**		
US	*0.36*	-0.03	*0.04*	-0.24	-0.16	0.30	0.50	*0.28*	**0.82**	
VP	0.22	0.16	-0.13	*0.21*	-0.41	*0.22*	0.64	*0.30*	0.35	**0.98**

Notes. (1) Diagonal elements are the square root of average variance extracted (AVE). These values should exceed the interconstruct correlations for adequate discriminant validity. (2) The italic values show correlations included in our structural models. (3) NA - Does not apply for formative measures.

Table 8.7.: Latent Variable Correlations for Interpretation Scenarios

level of 0.05 cannot be rejected.

Consequently, it is assumed that these paths are not empirically explaining the research model. H6b and H7b are not supported empirically. MA has a weak negative impact on EY (beta=-0.116, $f2=0.01$, $p<0.05$). This relation is not contributing to H8b. As a consequence it can be stated, that in the modeling domain MA is negatively influencing the time used for model interpretation. PA is positively influencing EY (beta=0.435, $f2=0.24$, $p<0.001$) and US (beta=0.280, $f2=0.075$, $p<0.05$). Users ability of complete and correct model interpretation is positively influencing US (beta=0.362, $f2=0.11$, $p<0.01$). From this it is deduced that H9b is accepted.

Turning to model fit, the R-square values for MA, LA, EY, ES, US and PA were 0.473, 0.202, 0.194, 0.420, 0.192 and 0.196 respectively, indicating that the model explains substantial variation in these variables. The results show that most hypotheses in this research model are fully supported. However, H8b is not supported by our results. Furthermore, H6b, H7b and H13b could not be confirmed by significant results.

As a consequence, particular hypotheses are not confirmed for further comparable samples. The resulting regression weights of H6b, H7b and H13b are valid for the specific sample and should be proved in further surveys based on this research model.

8.2.4. Analyzing Causal Paths in the Research Model

Table 8.8 shows assumed causal relations and marked significant paths in interpretation scenarios based on the empirical results. The findings described in this section underline the general

No.	Path
1	$VP \rightarrow LA \rightarrow ES \rightarrow US$
2	$VP \rightarrow PA \rightarrow US$
3	$LC \rightarrow PA \rightarrow US$

Table 8.8.: Causal Paths in Interpretation Scenarios

hypothesis that Visual Properties and Language Complexity both set in language's metamodel act as exogenous latent variables in the research model.

Causal Path 1 This path shows, that multiple colors and geometric shapes (VP) in language's metamodel support LA of interpreting models developed with particular language. Consequently, a possible theoretical reason is that various colors and shapes lead to more information structuredness supporting learnability of interpreting models [Hall and Hanna, 2004]. Compared to model development tasks LA is supporting user's ability accomplishing tasks completely and accurately. In former findings of cognitive psychology low gradients of learning curves causes ineffective application of a construct in a specific domain [Anderson, 1985]. Finally, high ES-values result in high US-values. From this path can be deduced that languages offering multiple colors and geometric shapes support LA, ES consequently US.

Causal Path 2 In interpretation scenarios we additionally introduced visual Perceptibility (PA) as latent variable for defining usability. The results underline the assumption that PA is a basic variable for measuring usability in model interpretation tasks. Multiple colors and geometrics in language's metamodel support the perceptibility of modeling languages. A theoretic fundament can be deduced by using findings of Hall and Hanna (2004) again. Their findings have to be applied in interpretation scenarios at concrete model level by concluding that models containing various colors and geometric shapes support user's cognitive processes (i.e. information search, information extraction, information processing). Furthermore, PA leads to higher values in US. Many researchers concluded a strong impact of design (screen, website etc.) and especially layout and order of elements on target individual's satisfaction [De Angeli et al., 2006, Sonderegger and Sauer, 2009]. Lindgaard (2007) states a positive link between user satisfaction and visual screen design [Lindgaard, 2007].

Causal Path 3 This path is characterized by the positive effect of low level of language complexity (LC) on PA. Consequently it is deduced that PA is not only impacted by VP but also by LC. This result contributes to Pan et al. (2004). They analyze the viewing behavior of web pages by using an eye-tracker [Pan et al., 2004]. They concluded that visual complexity negatively contributes to eye-movement behavior due to difficulty of information search and information extraction. It is concluded, that languages offering high metamodel complexity (i.e.

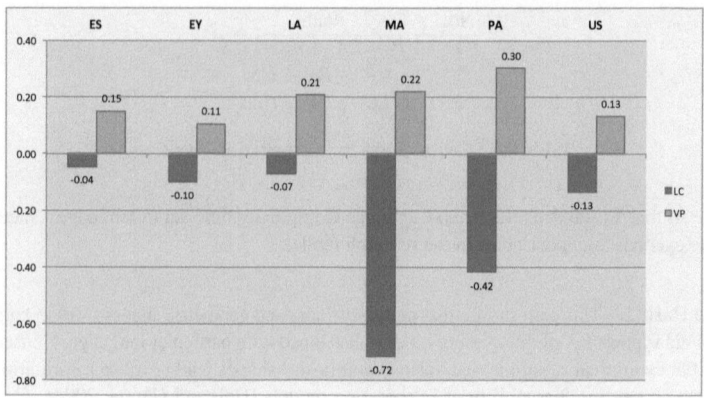

Figure 8.2.4.: Total Effects in Interpretation Scenarios

UML-Class Diagrams etc.) complicate user's ability of searching, extracting and processing information in model interpretation tasks.

8.2.5. Total Effects of Metaproperties

After calculating the total effects of usability impacting metaproperties of modeling languages, it is possible to analyze the total impact of variations of LC and VP on each usability attribute. For each usability attribute the standardized total effects of LC and VP are shown in Figure 8.2.4 :

First, this analysis shows that the complexity of language's metamodel influences all defined usability attributes negatively. In general, this means that the relation between language complexity and the defined usability attributes is inverse. Consequently, increasing language complexity by e.g. adding elements and relations influences all defined usability attributes negatively. Concerning this, memorability is influenced most by complexity rise (-0.72).

Another interesting finding is that an effective task accomplishment (ES) is comparable low caused by language complexity (-0.04) in interpretation scenarios. Furthermore, the total effect of language complexity on learnability is comparable low (-0.07). On the other side, the total effect of language complexity rise on perceptibility is comparable high (-0.42). This means that user's ability of searching and extracting information out of a model diagram falls short if language complexity rises.

Second, for visual properties (VP), the total effect on the defined usability attributes is in all cases positive. It becomes obvious that the total effect variance of VP between usability attributes is not as high as LC.

Finally, providing visual differentiation by applying multiple colors and shapes supports visual perceptibility most.

8.2.6. Discussion for Model Interpretation Scenarios

From the results it is deduced that the complexity of language's metamodel, i.e. variability in elements, relations and properties, is strongly influencing user's ability to remember them. Usability research shows that memorability is an initial basis for applying a system or a website effectively [18]. However, the theses for the model interpretation scenario cannot be confirmed with the results.

Memorability is weakly influencing effectiveness of model interpretation. Furthermore, memorability is weakly influencing effectiveness and that memorability weakly impacts interpretation time negatively. It seems that these research findings for the causal path between memorability and efficiency of model interpretation remain inconclusive. Concerning this, further research into this area will be required and may lead to more conclusive findings. However, it seems that memorability plays a secondary role in model interpretation scenario.

Besides, metamodel complexity is strongly influencing language's visual perceptibility. This result provides evidence that languages based on complex metamodels are not supporting user's ability of easy information search and extraction when interpreting a model. Additionally the visual perceptibility of modeling languages is strongly connected with duration time of information search and extraction. Concerning this, it is deduced that languages offering a good perceptibility afford fast information search and information extraction times leading to an efficient model interpretation process.

Moreover, the visual perceptibility of a modeling language is positively supporting user's individual language satisfaction. From this result it can be deduced that visual perceptibility is one important base of user satisfaction. User acceptance is strongly connected with user satisfaction [Nielsen, 2006b]. This relationship underlines the fact that visual perceptibility concerning particular languages is obviously a basic result of user satisfaction and consequently user acceptance. In other words, visual perceptibility may decide whether a modeling language is accepted or not by users concerning model interpretation. Obviously, the positive impact of interpretation time on user satisfaction is not as much as expected. Similar to the model development scenario, this might be underlining former findings of Walker (1998). In their studies they found out that users have demonstrated preferences for systems with which they performed less efficiently [Walker et al., 1998]. It shows that the ability for finishing interpretation tasks completely and correctly and the ability for convenient information search and information extraction out of a model are more important to satisfy users than the commonly assumed performance factors of efficiency.

An important result of our survey is the causal impact of visual language properties, i.e. variability in shape geometrics and shape colors, in the field of model interpretation. The output of our study shows that visual language properties are positively influencing the visual perceptibility of modeling languages. This result underlines the finding that visual differentiation supports object information search and information extraction [Westphal and Würtz, 2009].

As a consequence, the application of different colors and geometrics in a model supports interpreting users in searching and extracting information. Furthermore the variability in shape color and geometrics is positively influencing learnability of model interpretation and memorability of language's elements and relations. Consequently, languages offering higher variability in geometrics and colors are easier to learn concerning model interpretation. The learnability of interpreting a model based on a certain language is strongly impacting the ability of performing an interpretation task completely and correctly. For example, in industry and education it is important that users can interpret developed models with a high level of completeness and correctness [Mendling and Strembeck, 2008].

This study shows that learnability, which is positively influenced by visual language properties acts as a basic independent variable strongly impacting on user's ability of complete and correct model interpretation. Furthermore, learnability is positively influencing efficiency of model interpretation. In conclusion, learnability is a basic construct in model interpretation scenarios. A theoretical basis might be cognitive load theory and especially intrinsic cognitive load [Sweller, 2005]. The intrinsic cognitive load is determined by information complexity. The interdependency of information to be learned is positively impacting cognitive load and consequently the more important learnability appears in a causal system. Concerning modeling languages and model interpretation, the cognitive load is high because of strong information interdependency occurring in models. Considering our results and cognitive load theory the importance of learnability in model interpretation is emphasized.

In due consideration of our results it consequently becomes clear that learnability is positively impacted by visual language properties. From this follows that languages offering high visual variability are easier to learn than other. As a consequence languages containing high visual variability allow higher task completion and accuracy rates in model interpretation. In conclusion, if a language should support effectiveness of model interpretation, the metamodel should offer high visual variability in elements and relations. Concerning this, the complexity of language's metamodel is not determining language support of effectiveness in model interpretation.

Part III.

RESUME OF THE EMPIRICAL RESULTS

9. Further Processing of the Empirical Results

This chapter offers a further processing of the findings explored in the empirical surveys. In detail, the dimensions of modeling, the target conflict of modeling and the modeling process are introduced and updated under consideration of the empirical findings of this thesis. Furthermore, a decision framework for IT managers focusing on the selection of suitable modeling languages considering usability criteria is developed. Finally, concluding usability oriented principles for the further development of modeling languages are defined. In general, this chapter shows how the empirical findings are applied to optimize the modeling domain in theory and practice.

9.1. Dimensions of Modeling

In companies, the importance of software and business process modeling has steadily risen. Consequently, the development and interpretation of models become an issue of organizational concerns. The question of how efficiently can models be developed or interpreted may be very interesting for CIOs in modern enterprises.

Pohl (1994) defined three goals of modeling in enterprises [Pohl, 1994]:

- improving an opaque domain comprehension into a complete domain specification
- transforming informal knowledge into formal representations
- gaining a common agreement on the domain specification out of the personal views

Out of these goals, three dimensions of modeling can be gained: specification, representation and agreement dimension.

The *specification dimension* deals with the degree of process understanding at a given time. At the beginning of the modeling procedure the specification of the domain modelled and its environment is more or less opaque. Focusing on this dimension, the aim of a model is to transform the operational need into a complete specification through an iterative process of definition and validation.

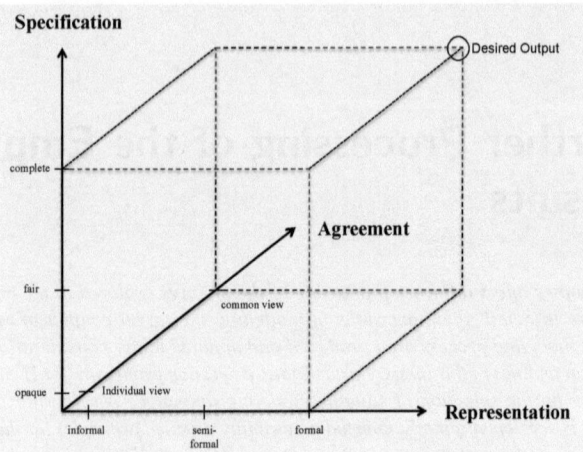

Figure 9.1.1.: Three Dimensions of Modeling

The *representation dimension* copes with the different representations (informal and formal languages, shapes, colors) used for expressing knowledge about the process.

The *agreement dimension* deals with the degree of agreement reached on a specification. At the beginning of the modeling procedure each person involved has its own personal view of the domain modelled. For example, a few steps of a business process may be shared among the team at this stage, but the whole business process including activities, states, organization units etc. exist only within personal views of the people stemming from the various roles they have (business analyst, manager, user, developer etc.).

9.2. Target Conflict of Modeling

Considering the modeling process and related users of modeling languages, a goal conflict between the usability of a modeling language and the specification and representation dimensions appears. The awareness of this goal conflict is justified with the empirical results of the surveys conducted in this thesis.

The general empirical result based on the surveys of this thesis is that

(1) usability is influenced negatively by language complexity

(2) usability is influenced positively by visual properties of a modeling language

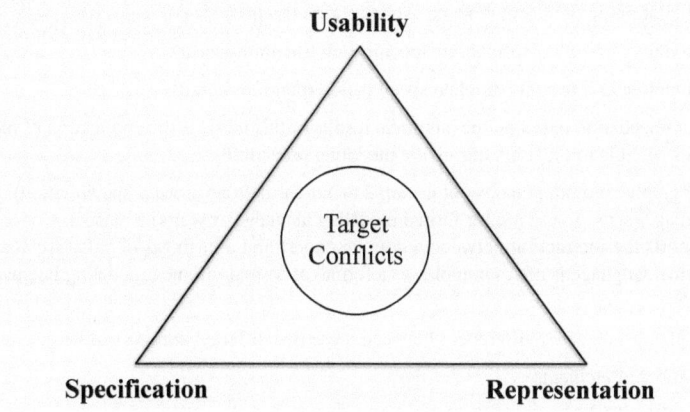

Figure 9.2.1.: Target Conflict of Modeling

The ability of a formal representation and complete specification increases the complexity of a modeling language compared to informal representations and opaque specifications.

The outcome of these relationships is a goal conflict between usability and the dimensions of specification and representation.

9.3. Adoption of the Modeling Process

The target conflicts of modeling and the different modeling dimensions in the classical information modeling process influence an adoption of the modeling process.

In order to initiate the information modeling process the business analyst or software engineer must elicit a process or system specification from domain experts. In this phase domain knowledge is gathered in interactive sessions with domain experts and business/software analysts. The elicitation results in an informal specification (also referred to as the requirements document). As natural language is humans essential vehicle to convey ideas, this requirements document is written in natural language.

In case of an evolutionary development, the previous requirements document will be used as a starting point for the development of models [Frederiks and van der Weide, 2006].

More advance in the modeling process leads to technical and formal accomplished users (e.g. developer, business analyst, system engineer etc.). Consequently, the proposed modeling process and connected major steps based on the empirical results in this thesis are as follows:

1. Elicitation of an informal/opaque specification (textual)

2. Modeling of a semi-formal/fair specification (diagram-based)

3. Modeling of a formal/complete specification (diagram-based)

The recommendation based on the empirical results of this thesis is the application of modeling languages suitable to the users during the modeling procedure.

The first graphical model comes out in step 2 (semi-formal/fair process specification). On this stage it makes sense to use a semi-formal modeling language as well (i.e. EPCs). Consequently, this supports the interaction between a domain expert and a business or software analyst. A semi-formal language is not as complex as a formal or formal-oriented modeling language such as BPMN.

In particular, user-related differences between those two different concepts of languages are:

- number of elements
- number of relations
- number of properties

In other words, the user-related differences between semi-formal and formal modeling languages is their complexity.

In most cases a domain expert has no or weak experiences in the application of graphical modeling languages. The confrontation of domain experts with a language that is usable is more efficient in the modeling process.

The reason for that is based in the empirical results of this thesis.

A novice has to learn the application of a modeling language effectively and efficiently, has to memorize the different elements and relations and, finally, has to be satisfied with the application of that language. Consequently, it makes sense

1. to confront beginners with modeling languages suitable to their skills or

2. reduce/raise language complexity suitable to user skills.

9.4. Recommendations for Future Improvement of graphical Modeling Languages

The empirical results of chapter 6 show that EPCs, a language for modeling business processes, offer the best usability in this survey.

In companies the importance of business process modeling has steadily risen. Consequently, the development and interpretation of models become an issue of organizational concerns.

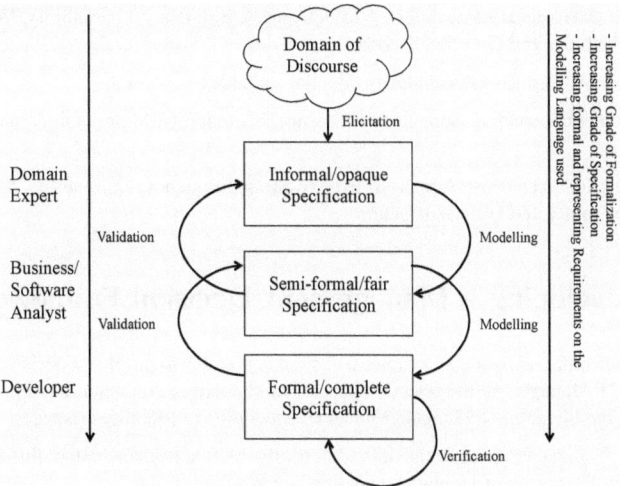

Figure 9.3.1.: Proposed Process of Modeling

For the model interpretation scenario, questions such as whether employees understand the information modelled do appear. Thus, companies aiming for fast, complete and correct model interpretation, e.g. business process consulting companies, typically apply modeling languages offering high variability in visual properties. In many cases those companies customize languages such as the BPMN by

1. adding colors or shapes to support complete and accurate model interpretation.

2. reducing language complexity (i.e. element limitation) to support the user in model interpretation and model development scenarios

Since EPCs offer highest usability values in development and interpretation scenarios, the empirical results support this course of action.

Recommendations

The recommendations for the future improvement of graphical modeling languages based on the empirical results of this thesis are as follows:

R1) Enrichment of the metamodel with color and shape information

⇒ Development Scenarios: Support of Effectiveness, Efficiency and Learnability

⇒ Interpretation Scenarios: Support of Effectiveness, Efficiency, Learnability, Memorability, Perceptibility and User Satisfaction

R2) Complexity Reduction/Complexity adoption suitable to user skills

⇒ Development Scenarios: Support of Efficiency, Learnability, Memorability and User Satisfaction

⇒ Interpretation Scenarios: Support of Effectiveness, Efficiency, Learnability, Memorability, Perceptibility and User Satisfaction

9.5. Developing a Management Decision Framework

Based on the empirical results of chapter 6 and 8 it is possible to develop a decision framework supporting IT Managers in the selection process of choosing a suitable modeling language or customized modification of a language under consideration of usability aspects.

In the case of language customization it is additionally referred to chapter 10 of this thesis, where principles for the design of graphical modeling languages are given.

The framework is structured in several sections expressed by decision nodes. The first decision node distinguishes between the specific scenario, which is applied predominantly in a specific company. The second distinction is made between the particular usability attributes that are focused on.

At this stage the decider has two possibilities: First, a suitable language is chosen and second an existing language is customized under consideration of the specific recommendations.

Figure 9.5.1 shows the developed decision framework based on the empirical results of the research presented in this thesis.

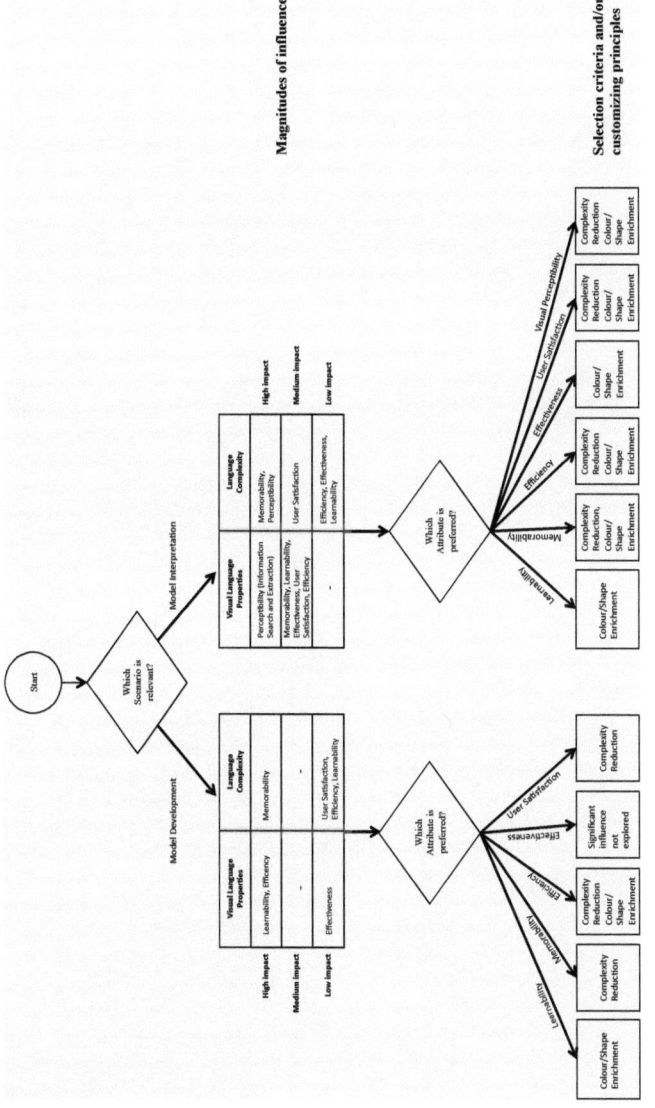

Figure 9.5.1.: Management Decision Framework

10. Principles for Future Development of graphical Modeling Languages

This chapter defines a set of principles based on the empirical results of this thesis and on current literature. As shown in the empirical surveys, two major criteria of graphical modeling languages influence the usability and connected attributes significantly:

- Visual properties
- Language complexity

Based on the empirical surveys of this thesis, the general finding is that the enlargement of visual properties supports the usability of the four modeling languages in development and interpretation scenarios. The question that has to be asked at this stage is what are principles when designing visual properties in graphical modeling languages. Researchers such as Moody (2010) analyzed this issue and with the survey results his general ideas and theses are confirmed. In the following chosen visual principles for designing graphical modeling languages are presented.

10.1. Principle of Semiotic Clarity

This principle focuses on the fact that there must be a one to one correspondence between graphical shapes/colors and their referent semantic concepts. When a one to one correspondence between constructs and symbols doesn't exist, one or more of the following anomalies may occur:

- *symbol redundancy* occurs when multiple graphical shapes/colors represent the same semantic construct
- *symbol overload* occurs when two different semantic constructs are represented by one graphical shape/color
- *symbol excess* occurs when graphical shapes/colors do not correspondent to any semantic construct
- *symbol deficit* occurs when semantic constructs exist without being represented by graphical shapes/colors

10.2. Principle of Visual Discriminability

Perceptual discriminability is the ease and accuracy with which graphical symbols can be differentiated from each other. Accurate discrimination between symbols is an essential issue for efficient interpretation of models. The following criteria are relevant for ensuring visual discriminability:

- *visual distance* between different shapes/colors
- *primacy of shapes*: geometrics represent the primary basis on which we identify objects in the real world
- *redundant coding* increases visual discriminability: using multiple visual shapes/colors to distinguish between them
- *perceptual pop-out*: each graphical shape/color should have a unique value on at least one visual variable

10.3. Principle of Semantic Transparency

Semantic transparency is defined as the extent to which the meaning of a symbol can be inferred from its appearance. While perceptual discriminability simply requires that shapes/colors should be different from each other, this principle requires that they provide cues to their meaning:

- a symbol is *semantically immediate* if a novice reader would be able to infer its meaning from its appearance alone (e.g. a user in UML Use Case diagrams)
- a symbol is *semantically opaque* if there is a purely arbitrary relationship between its appearance and its meaning (e.g. rectangles in Entity Relationship diagrams)
- a symbol is *semantically perverse* if a novice user (interpreter or developer) would be likely to infer a different meaning from its appearance.

10.4. Principle of Complexity Management

Complexity management refers to the ability of a visual notation to represent information without overloading the human mind. On the one hand the complexity of the language i.e. semantics and syntax and on the other hand visual issues such as shapes and colors can overload the human brain.

One result of the studies presented in this thesis is that complexity has a major effect on usability and connected attributes as the amount of information that can be effectively conveyed by a single model is limited by human perceptual and cognitive abilities. Considering the following recommendations in further language development or language customization activities lead to a usability-oriented complexity management with particular modeling languages:

- *Perceptual limits:* The ability to discriminate between diagram elements increases with diagram size
- *Cognitive limits:* The number of diagram elements and syntactic regulations that can be comprehended at a time is limited by working-memory capacity. When this is exceeded, a state of cognitive overload ensues and comprehension degrades rapidly

10.5. Principle of Visual Expressiveness

Visual expressiveness is defined as the number of visual variables used in a notation. This principle is mainly important for supporting the usability of graphical modeling languages in mode interpretation scenarios. The use of the following variables supports the visual expressiveness of a model that was developed by using a certain modeling language:

- use of color
- use of size
- use of brightness
- use of geometric shapes

10.6. Principle of Dual Coding

Using text and graphics together to convey information is more effective than using either on their own. When information is presented both verbally and visually, representations of that information are encoded in separate systems in working memory and referential connections between the two are strengthened. This suggests that textual encoding is most effective when it is used in a supporting role: to supplement rather than to substitute for graphics.

- annotations such as multiplicities in UML Class Diagrams
- hybrid symbols such as multiplicities in UML CLass Diagrams in conjunction with different relationship types (aggregation, composition etc.)

10.7. Principle of Graphic Economy

Graphic complexity is defined by the number of graphical symbols in a notation. Graphic complexity affects novices much more than experts, as they need to consciously maintain meanings of symbols in working memory.

The human ability to discriminate between perceptually distinct alternatives (span of absolute judgment) is around six categories: This defines an upper limit for graphic complexity. Many graphical modeling languages exceed this limit by an order of magnitude: For example, UML Class Diagrams have a graphic complexity of over 40 and BPMN 2.0 of over 160.

There are three main strategies for dealing with excessive graphic complexity [Moody and Heymans, 2010]:

- reduce semantic complexity
- introduce symbol deficit
- increase visual expressiveness

10.8. Principle of Cognitive Fit

Cognitive fit theory is a widely accepted theory in the information systems field that has been validated in a wide range of domains, from managerial decision making to program maintenance [Shaft and Vessey, 2006].

The theory states that different representations of information are suitable for different tasks and different users. Problem solving performance is determined by a three-way fit between the problem representation, task characteristics, and problem solver skills.

However, cognitive fit theory suggests that this "one size fits all" assumption may be inappropriate and different visual dialects may be required for different tasks and/or audiences. These represent complementary rather than competing visual dialects as discussed earlier.

There are at least two reasons for creating multiple visual dialects:

- *Expert-novice differences*: problem solver skills
- *Representational medium*: task characteristics

Part IV.

CONCLUSION AND OUTLOOK

11. Conclusion

In this thesis an empirical usability evaluation of four graphical modeling languages in business process and software modeling was conducted.

First, the theoretical background of usability in the domain of graphical modeling languages was deduced.

Based on this, a framework for usability evaluation of graphical modeling languages (FUEML) was developed.

In the next step, the framework was applied in two empirical surveys analyzing the usability of four graphical modeling languages.

In the following the most important results and findings of the research conducted in this thesis are summarized. The FUEML framework and the findings of the empirical surveys offer answers to all research questions defined in chapter one figure 1.1.

11.1. The FUEML Evaluation Framework

The theoretical background of the modeling and usability area was analyzed and consequently applied for the development of an usability evaluation framework for graphical modeling languages (FUEML). FUEML gives answers to the research questions Q3, Q5 and Q6 (see figure 1.1).

This framework includes the following constituent parts:

Different User Scenarios

Considering the user of modeling languages, each user can be exposed to different situations. Some may be primarily involved with the **development of models**, while others may be primarily involved with the **interpretation of models** [Siau and Wang, 2007].

This criterion is considered in FUMEL and consequently in the empirical surveys conducted within the research described in this thesis.

Relevant Usability Attributes

With analyzing basic usability literature and standards it was possible to deduce relevant usability attributes for the domain of graphical modeling languages. In conclusion those attributes are

- Learnability
- Memorability
- Effectiveness
- Efficiency
- User Satisfaction

The attributes are applicable for both model development and model interpretation scenarios. In addition to that, a sixth attributes was introduced for the particular scenario of model interpretation. Visual characteristics of models developed by the application of specific languages are considered within the attribute of

- Visual Perceptibility

Relevant Usability Metrics

For making the different usability attributes measurable, concrete metrics depending on the restrictive investigation object were defined. The metrics are either basically functions that are defined in terms of a formula or simple countable data. Furthermore, a questionnaire was developed for measuring the individual satisfaction of a user. For measuring the individual remembering rate of a user a knowledge test was developed.

Control Variables in this Domain

For the development of a usability evaluation framework it is important to consider control variables i.e. variables that interfere the data output and therefore has to be controlled. In FUEML

- Prior Knowledge and
- Model Complexity

are analyzed as control variables.

Prior knowledge comprises the individual experience of a survey participant. For example, the times for a development or an interpretation task of users with differing grades of modeling experience are not directly comparable. Therefore, the individual experience is tracked and consequently the task times are adjusted considering participant's experience.

Due to the fact that the survey conducted in this research crosses over several modeling languages, the different task complexities (i.e. model complexity) have to be calculated. Consequently, the data output has to be adjusted considering the criterion of model complexity.

Language-based Metaproperties influencing Usability

The pivotal question in the FUEML framework focuses on different metaproperties of modeling languages, which impact the usability attributes. After analyzing the structure and the design of graphical modeling languages the following metaproperties were concluded:

- Language Complexity
- Visual Properties

Language complexity is measured by the number of different elements, the number of different relations and the number of different properties.

The visual properties of graphical modeling languages can be concluded by the number of different shapes and the number of different colors set in the metamodel of the specific modeling language.

11.2. The Empirical Section

Based on this, several hypothesis assuming differences of various modeling languages regarding their impact on usability are developed. Subsequently, the defined hypotheses are explored by the conduction of an empirical survey. The data analysis is calculated by using an

- Analysis of Covariance (ANCOVA) and a
- Structural Equation Modeling (SEM) approach

for analyzing causal interactions and relations between language and usability attributes.

For the conducted ANCOVA the FUEML framework and the developed metrics are applied without any changes. The output is a empirical-based comparison of analyzed modeling languages regarding their usability.

For the SEM analysis, usability and connected attributes are set in a model containing causal hypotheses and interactions between them. The output of this analysis has a causal character i.e. it is analyzed how different metaproperties of graphical modeling languages influence usability on different causal stages. For example, it is explored how the use of colors and shapes in the metamodel of modeling languages impact different usability attributes.

11.3. General Findings of this Thesis

The general findings of the research conducted in this thesis are based on the results of the empirical chapters. The findings offer answers to the research questions Q1, Q2 and Q4 (see figure 1.1)

- Usability-influencing metaproperties of graphical modeling languages are elements, relations, properties, shapes and colors. These properties are language-specific→Q4
- Different modeling concepts influence the usability in different ways →Q1

  – The classification of the four analyzed languages shows that process-based languages are more usable than structure-based modeling languages.

  – The classification of the four analyzed languages shows that languages offering high visual differentiation properties such as different shapes and colors in the metamodel are more usable than languages offering low visual differentiation properties.

  – The classification of the four analyzed languages shows that complex modeling languages are not as usable as simple modeling languages.

- Visual Properties have a positive effect on usability attributes whereas language complexity has a negative influence on usability attributes →Q2
- The causal influence of language metaproperties (i.e. elements, relations, properties, shapes and colors) on the usability attributes is not uniformly distributed. The grade of influence depends on the specific user scenario and the particular usability attribute →Q2

Based on the findings of the empirical surveys it is possible to conclude two basic usability-supporting recommendations for the further development of graphical modeling languages:

- Enrichment of the metamodel with color and shape information
- Complexity reduction/adoption suitable to user skills

Under consideration of the fact that complexity reduction of modeling languages possibly may impact the expense of explanatory power these recommendations may also be applied for customizing existing graphical modeling languages in enterprises.

Furthermore, the empirical results are transferred to business practice including the

- proposal of an modeling process in enterprises considering the empirical results of this thesis (see chapter 9.3) and
- the development of a management decision framework supporting the usability-oriented selection of graphical modeling languages in enterprises (see chapter 9.5).

11.4. Threats to External Validity

External validity is the extent to which the findings can be legitimately generalized. Experts identified several threats to external validity such as experimental effects, novelty effects ot taks effects [Mitchell and Jolley, 2001].

For the research conducted and presented in this thesis it is essential to define the following threats to the generalization of the empirical results.

Since the data collection focuses on student groups, a design effect can be defined as threat to external validity. Generally, the results of this thesis are just relevant for novices of modeling. General deductions to industry and experts in industry cannot be made by the empirical results of this thesis. However, the general direction of the influence of modeling languages on different usability attributes can be deduced externally. Concerning this, it is important to mention that I strongly recommend further research in this domain for confirming my hypotheses and extending my empirical results.

Another significant threat to external validity is the influence of the modeling tool on the calculated usability metrics based on the empirical data material. For further studies I highly recommend the use of ArgoUML or the Bflow-Toolbox for ensuring the comparability to my results. If this is not possible, the results of further studies cannot be compared to my results directly.

Future studies should also include further modeling languages for extending and confirming my results. Consequently, it could be possible to generalize my findings to the entire domain of graphical modeling languages.

12. Outlook

The research documented in this thesis has drawn on a wide range of modeling language and usability theories to produce a new framework for usability evaluation of graphical modeling languages.

Past and current research highlighted the need to deal with a usability survey focusing on graphical modeling languages. The research presented in this thesis has both practical and theoretical use.

The theoretical use focuses on researchers of the modeling domain and the usability domain. In the modeling domain, the developed FUEML evaluation framework and the findings of this thesis act as a basis for forthcoming usability surveys. In the usability domain the developed causal models including several causal stages connecting usability attributes may be interesting for further research activites. Current usability investigations only set the different usability attributes on one causal level.

The practical use focuses on standardization organizations such as the ISO and enterprises. The results of the empirical findings support standardization organizations developing graphical modeling languages in considering usability aspects for the further development of graphical modeling languages. For example, a possible requirement deduced from the findings of this thesis may be the adaptability of graphical modeling languages suitable to user's experience regarding the complexity and the visual properties of the modeling language. However, this step would require further empirical investigations of how language complexity and visual properties influence users with differing grades of language experiences.

The developed FUEML evaluation framework and the findings of this thesis act as a basis for forthcoming surveys in this domain. For confirming and extending the empirical results of this thesis it is recommended for further research to integrate different modeling languages and practitioner groups in the surveys. This is necessary for showing a general validity of the results presented in this research. The results of further studies cannot be compared directly with the results of this research unless further studies consider similar modeling tools for the development scenarios and student groups.

In summary, it can be said that this thesis forms a solid foundation of usability in the domain of graphical modeling languages and should be seen as a starting point for further continuous usability investigations of graphical modeling languages.

A. Appendix (online supplement)

This appendix is available at Springer Gabler OnlinePlus:

www.springer-gabler.de/Buch/978-3-658-00050-9/usability-evaluation-of-modeling-languages.html

Bibliography

[Abran et al., 2003] Abran, A., Khelifi, A., Suryn, W., and Seffah, A. (2003). Consolidating the iso usability models.

[Abrial, 1974] Abrial, J.-R. (1974). Data semantics. In Klimbie, J. and Koffman, J., editors, *Data Management Systems*, pages 1–59. North Holland.

[Ambler, 2005] Ambler, S. W. (2005). *The elements of UML 2.0 style*. Cambridge University Press.

[Anderson, 1985] Anderson, J. (1985). *Cognitive psychology and its implications*. Freeman, New York, 2 edition.

[Angles and Guteierrez, 2008] Angles, R. and Guteierrez, C. (2008). Survey on graph database models. *Computing Surveys*, 40(1):25–46.

[Armstrong et al., 2005] Armstrong, D., Gogarty, G., Dingsdag, D., and Dimbley, J. (2005). Validation of a computer user satisfaction questionnaire validation of a computer user satisfaction questionnaire to measure is success in small business. *Journal of Research and Practice in Information Technology*, 37(1):22–38.

[Arnesen and Krogstie, 2005] Arnesen, S. and Krogstie, J. (2005). Assessing enterprise modeling languages using a generic quality framework. In Krogstie John, Halpin Terry A., S. K., editor, *Information Modeling Methods and Methodologies*, pages 63–79. Hershey PA: Idea Group.

[Atkinson and Kuhne, 2003] Atkinson, C. and Kuhne, T. (2003). Model-driven development: a metamodeling foundation. *IEEE Software*, 20(5):36–41.

[Avison and Fitzgerald, 1995] Avison, D. and Fitzgerald, G. (1995). *Information Systems Development: Methodologies, Techniques and Tools*. McGraw-Hill Book Company, New York.

[Barbier and Henderson-Sellers, 2000] Barbier, F. and Henderson-Sellers, B. (2000). Object modelling languages: An evaluation and some key expectations for the future. *Ann. Softw. Eng.*, 10(1-4):67–101.

[Barker et al., 1994] Barker, C., Pistrang, N., and Elliott, R. (1994). *Reserach methods in clinical and counseling psychology*. John Wiley, Chichester.

[Batra and Davis, 1992] Batra, D. and Davis, J. (1992). Conceptual data modeling in database design: Similarities and differences between expert and novice designers. *Inernational Journal of Man-Machine Studies*, 37(1):83–101.

[Belady and Evangelisti, 1981] Belady, L. A. and Evangelisti, C. J. (1981). System partitioning and its measure. *Journal of Systems and Software*, 2(1):23–29.

[Bertin, 1983] Bertin, J. (1983). *Semiology of graphics: diagrams, networks, maps*. University of Wisconsin Press, Madison.

[Bevan, 1995] Bevan, N. (1995). Measuring usability as quality of use. *Software Quality Journal*, 4:115–150.

[Bevan and Macleod, 1994] Bevan, N. and Macleod, M. (1994). Usability measurment in context. *Behaviour and Information Technology*, 13(1):132–145.

[Birkmeier et al., 2010] Birkmeier, D., Klöckner, S., and Overhage, S. (2010). An empirical comparison of the usability of bpmn and uml activity diagrams for business users. In *Proceedings of the 18th European Conference on Information Systems (ECIS)*, South Africa.

[Blalock, 1982] Blalock, H. M. (1982). *Conceptualization and Measurement in the Social Sciences*. SAGE Publications.

[Blanthorne et al.,] Blanthorne, C., Jones-Farmer, A., and Almer, E. D. Why you should consider sem: A guide to getting started. In Schmitt, D. B., editor, *Advances in Accounting Behavioral Research*, volume 9, pages 179–207. Emerald Group Publishing Limited.

[Bobkowska, 2005a] Bobkowska, A. (2005a). A framework for methodologies of visual modeling language evaluation. *ACM International Conference Proceeding Series*, 214(2).

[Bobkowska, 2005b] Bobkowska, A. (2005b). Modeling pragmatics for visual modeling language evaluation (tamodia '05). In *Proceedings of the 4th Workshop on Task Models and Diagrams*, volume 127, Gdansk.

[Bock, 1975] Bock, R. (1975). *Multivariate statistical Methods in behavioural Research*. McGraw-Hill Book Company.

[Bodart et al., 2001] Bodart, F., Patel, A., Sim, M., and Weber, R. (2001). Should optional properties be used in conceptual modelling? a theory and three empirical tests. *Information Systems Research*, 12(1):384–405.

[Booch et al., 1998] Booch, G., Rumbaugh, J., and Jacobson, I. (1998). *The Unified Modeling Language User Guide*. Addison-Wesley Professional.

[Bresciani et al., 2004] Bresciani, P., Perini, A., Giorgini, P., Giunchiglia, F., and Mylopoulos, J. (2004). Tropos: An agent-oriented software development methodology. *Autonomous Agents and Multi-Agent Systems*, 8(3):203–236.

[Bubenko, 1986] Bubenko, J. (1986). Information system methodologies; a research view.

[Burton et al., 2009] Burton, Jones, A., Wand, Y., and Weber, R. (2009). Guidelines for empirical evaluations of conceptual modeling grammar. *Journal of the Association for Information Systems*, 10(6):495.532.

[Byrne et al., 1999] Byrne, M. D., Anderson, J., Douglass, S., and Matessa, M. (1999). Eye tracking the visual search of click-down menus. In *Proceedings of CHI'99*, pages 402–409.

[Chen, 1976] Chen, P. P. (1976). The entity-relationship model: toward a unified view of data. *ACM Transactions on Database Systems*, 1(1):9–36.

[Chiese et al., 1979] Chiese, H., Spilich, G., and Voss, J. (1979). Acquisition of domain related information in relation to high and low domain knowledge. *Journal of Verbal Learning and Verbal Behavior*, 18(1):257–273.

[Chin et al., 1988] Chin, J., Diehl, V., and Norman, K. (1988). Development of an instrument measuring user satisfaction of the human-computer interface. *Proceedings of the SIGCHI conference on Human factors in computing systems*, pages 213–218.

[Chin, 1998] Chin, W. W. (1998). Issues and opinion on structural equation modeling. *MIS Quarterly*, 22(1):7–16.

[Chin and Lee, 2000] Chin, W. W. and Lee, M. (2000). A proposed model and measurement instrument for the formation of is satisfaction: the case of end-user computing satisfaction. In *International Conference on Information Systems (ICIS) Proceedings*, Brisbane.

[Chin et al., 2003] Chin, W. W., Marcolin, B. L., and Newsted, P. R. (2003). A partial least squares latent variable modeling approach for measuring interaction effects: Results from a monte carlo simulation study and an electronic–mail emotion/adoption study. *Information Systems Research*, 14(2):189–217.

[Chin and Newsted, 1999] Chin, W. W. and Newsted, P. R. (1999). Structural equation modeling analysis with small samples using partial least squares. In Hoyle, R., editor, *Statistical Strategies for Small Sample Research*. Sage Publications.

[Codd, 1970] Codd, E. (1970). A relational model of data for large shared data banks. *Communications of the ACM*, 13(6):377–387.

[Comber and Maltby, 1997] Comber, T. and Maltby, J. (1997). Layout complexity: does it measure usability?

[Constantine and Lockwood, 1999] Constantine, L. and Lockwood, L. (1999). *Software for Use: A practical Guide to the Models and Methods of Usage-Centered Design*. Addison-Wesley, New York.

[Cook and Campbell, 1979] Cook, T. and Campbell, D. (1979). *Quasi-Experimentation: Design and Analysis for Field Settings*. Rand McNally.

[Cooper and Schindler, 2005] Cooper, D. and Schindler, P. (2005). *Business Research Methods*. McGraw-Hill, New York.

[Coursaris and Kim, 2006] Coursaris, C. and Kim, D. (2006). A qualitative review of empirical mobile usability studies. In *Proceedings of the 12th Americas International Conference on Information Systems (AMCIS)*, pages 85–94.

[Cronbach, 1951] Cronbach, L. (1951). Coefficient alpha and the internal structure of tests. *Psychometrika*, 16(3):297–324.

[Crutch and Warrington, 2005] Crutch, S. and Warrington, E. (2005). Abstract and concrete concepts have structurally different representational frameworks. *Brain*, 128(1):615–627.

[Dahl and Nygaard, 1966] Dahl, O.-J. and Nygaard, K. (1966). Simula: an algol-based simulation language. *Commun. ACM*, 9:671–678.

[Dancey and Reidy, 2011] Dancey, C. P. and Reidy, J. (2011). *Statistics Without Maths for Psychology*. Prentice Hall, Harlow, 5th edition.

[Das et al., 2008] Das, S., McEwan, T., and Douglas, D. (2008). Using eye-tracking to evaluate label alignment in online forms. In *Proceedings of the 5th Nordic conference on Human-Computer-Interaction (NordiCHI08)*, pages 451–454. ACM.

[De Angeli et al., 2006] De Angeli, A., Sutcliffe, A., and Hartmann, J. (2006). Interaction, usability and aesthetics: what influences users' preferences? *Proceedings of the 6th conference on Designing Interactive systems*, pages 271–280.

[Diamantopoulos and Winklhofer, 2001] Diamantopoulos, A. and Winklhofer, H. (2001). Index construction with formative indicators: An alternative to scale development. *J. Mark. Res.*, 38(2):269–277.

[Diestel, 2005] Diestel, R. (2005). *Graph Theory (Graduate Texts in Mathematics)*. Springer, 3rd edition.

[Duchowski, 2007] Duchowski, A. T. (2007). *Eye Tracking Methodology - Theory and Practice*. Springer, New York, 2 edition.

[Dumas and Redish, 1999] Dumas, J. and Redish, J. (1999). *A practical guide to usability testing*. Greenwood Publishing Group, Westport, 2nd edition edition.

[Dumas et al., 2005] Dumas, M., Hofstede, A., and Russel, N. (2005). Pattern-based analysis of bpmn - an extensive evaluation of the control-flow, the data and the resource perspectives.

[Ehmke and Wilson, 2007] Ehmke, C. and Wilson, S. (2007). Identifying web usability problems from eye-tracking data. In *Proceedings of the 21st British HCI Group Annual Conference on People and Computers (BCS-HCI'07)*, pages 119–128. British Computer Society.

[Eloranta et al., 2006] Eloranta, L., Kallio, E., and Thero, I. (2006). A notation evaluation of bpmn and uml ad.

[Elsuwe and Schmedding, 2001] Elsuwe, H. and Schmedding, D. (2001). Metriken für uml-modelle. *Informatik Forschung und Entwicklung*, 18(1):22–31.

[Esswein et al., 2004] Esswein, W., Gehlert, A., and Seiffert, G. (2004). Towards a framework for model migration. *Advanced Information Systems Engineering, Proceedings*, 3084:463–476. Bah71 Times Cited:0 Cited References Count:23 Biomedical Sciences Instrumentation.

[Evermann and Wand, 2005] Evermann, J. and Wand, Y. (2005). Toward formalizing domain modeling semantics in language syntax. *IEEE Transactions on Software Engineering*, 31(1):21–37.

[Fabrigar et al., 1999] Fabrigar, L., Wegener, D., MacCallum, R., and Strahan, E. (1999). Evaluating the use of exploratory factor analysis in psychological research. *Psychological Methods*, 62(4):272–299.

[Figl et al., 2010] Figl, K., Mendling, J., Strembeck, M., and Recker, J. (2010). On the cognitive effectiveness of routing symbols in process modeling languages. *Springer Lecture Notes in Business Information Processing (LNBIP)*, 47(1).

[Fitts et al., 1950] Fitts, P., Jones, R., and Milton, J. (1950). Eye movements of aircraft pilots during instrument-landing approaches. *Aeronautical Engineering Review*, 9(2):24–29.

[Fornell and Bookstein, 1982] Fornell, C. and Bookstein, F. (1982). Two structural equation models: Lisrel and pls applied to consumer exit-voice theory. *Journal of Marketing Research*, 19(2):440–452.

[Fornell and Larcker, 1981] Fornell, C. and Larcker, D. F. (1981). Evaluating structural equation models with unobservable variables and measurment error. *Journal of Marketing Research*, 18(2):39–50.

[Frederiks and van der Weide, 2006] Frederiks, P. and van der Weide, T. (2006). Information modeling: The process and the required competencies of its participants. *Data and Knowledge Engineering*, 58(1):4–20.

[Gefen et al., 2000] Gefen, D., Straub, D. W., and Boudreau, M.-C. (2000). Structural equation modeling and regression: Guidelines for research practice. *Communications of the Association for Information Systems*, 4(7):22–56.

[Gemino and Wand, 2003] Gemino, A. and Wand, Y. (2003). Evaluationg modeling techniques based on models of learning. *Communications of the ACM*, 46(10):79–84.

[Gemino and Wand, 2004] Gemino, A. and Wand, Y. (2004). A framework for empirical evaluation of conceptual modeling techniques. *Requirements Engineering*, 9(4):248–260.

[Glass et al., 1972] Glass, G., Peckham, P., and Sanders, J. (1972). Consequences of failure to meet assumptions underlying the fixed effects analyses of variance and covariance. *Review of Educational Research*, 42(2):237–288.

[Goldberg and Kotval, 1999] Goldberg, J. and Kotval, X. (1999). Computer interface evaluation using eye movements: methods and constructs. *International Journal of Industrial Ergonomics*, 24(6):631–645.

[Gordon, 2004] Gordon, I. E. (2004). *Theories of visual perception*. Psychology Press, Hove, 3. ed. edition.

[Greenspan et al., 1994] Greenspan, S., Mylopoulos, J., and Borgida, A. (1994). On formal requirements modeling languages: Rml revisited. In *Proceedings of the 16th International Conference on Software Engineering*, ICSE 94, pages 135–147, Los Alamitos, CA, USA. IEEE Computer Society Press.

[Grossman et al., 2009] Grossman, T., Fitzmaurice, G., and Attar, R. (2009). A survey of software learnability: metrics, methodologies and guidelines.

[Gurr, 1999] Gurr, C. (1999). Effective diagrammatic communication: Syntactic, semantic and pragmatic issues. *Journal of Visual Languages and Computing*, 10(4):317–342.

[Hall and Hanna, 2004] Hall, R. and Hanna, P. (2004). The impact of web page text-background colour combinations on readability, retention, aesthetics and behavioural intention. *Behaviour and Information Technology*, 23(3):183–195.

[Halstead, 1977] Halstead, M. (1977). *Elements of Software Science (Operating and programming systems series)*. Elsevier Science Inc., New York.

[Hammer and McLeod, 1978] Hammer, M. and McLeod, D. (1978). The semantic data model: A modelling mechanism for database applicaitons. In *Proceedings of the 1978 ACM SIGMOD international conference on management of data*, pages 26–36.

[Havey, 2005] Havey, M. (2005). *Essential business process modeling*. O'Reilly, Beijing, 1. ed. edition.

[Henry and Kafura, 1981] Henry, S. and Kafura, D. (1981). Software structure metrics based on information flow. *IEEE Transactions on Software Engineering*, 7(5):510–518.

[Henseler et al., 2009] Henseler, J., Ringle, C. M., and Sinkovics, R. R. (2009). The use of partial least square path modeling in international marketing. In Sinkovics, R. R. and Ghauri, P., editors, *Advances in international marketing*, volume 20, pages 277–320. Bingley, London.

[Homburg and Giering, 2001] Homburg, C. and Giering, A. (2001). Personal characteristics as moderators of the relationship between customer satisfaction an loyaltya: An empirical analysis. *Psychology and Marketing*, 18(1):43–66.

[IEEE610.12-1990, 1990] IEEE610.12-1990 (1990). Standard glossary of software engineering terminology. Technical report, Institute of Electrical and Electronics Engineers.

[Ilomäki, 2008] Ilomäki, T. (2008). The usability of music theory software: The analysis of twelve-tone music as a case study. In *Computer Music Modeling and Retrieval. Sense of Sounds: 4th International Symposium, CMMR 2007, Lecture Notes in Computer Science (LNCS)*, pages 98–109. Springer-Verlag.

[Ince and Hekmatpur, 1988] Ince, D. and Hekmatpur, S. (1988). An approch to automated software design based on product metrics. *Software Engineering Journal*, 3(2):6–53.

[Indulska et al., 2009] Indulska, M., Zur Muehlen, M., and Recker, J. C. (2009). Measuring method complexity: The case of the business process modeling notation. property complexity.

[ISO/IEC9126-1:2001, 2004] ISO/IEC9126-1:2001 (2004). Software engineering - product quality; parts 1-4. Technical report, International Organization for Standardization.

[ISO/IEC9241-11, 1998] ISO/IEC9241-11 (1998). Ergonomic requirements for office work with visual display terminals (vdts); part 11: Guidance on usability. Technical report, International Organization for Standardization.

[ISO/IEC9241-110, 2006] ISO/IEC9241-110 (2006). Ergonomics of human-system-interaction; part 110: Dialogue principles. Technical report, International Organization for Standardization.

[Jöreskog, 1978] Jöreskog, K. G. (1978). Structural analysis of covariance and correlation matrices. *Psychometrika*, 43(3):443–473.

[Kaiser, 1974] Kaiser, H. (1974). An index of factorial simplicity. *Psychometrika*, 39(1):31–36.

[Kan, 2002] Kan, S. H. (2002). *Metrics and Models in Software Quality Engineering*. Addison-Wesley, Boston, 2nd edition edition.

[Karagiannis and Kühn, 2002] Karagiannis, D. and Kühn, H. (2002). Metamodeling platforms. *Lecture Notes in Computer Science*, 2455(1):182–197.

[Karn et al., 1999] Karn, Keith, S., Ellis, S., and Cornell, J. (1999). The hunt for usability: tracking eye movements. In *CHI '99 extended abstracts on Human factors in computing systems*, pages 173–173. ACM.

[Kintsch, 1998] Kintsch, W. (1998). *Comprehension: A Paradigm for Cognition*. Cambridge University Press, Cambridge, Melbourne.

[Kirakowski and Corbett, 1993] Kirakowski, J. and Corbett, M. (1993). Sumi: The software usability measurement inventory. *British Journal of Educational Technology*, 24(1):210–212.

[Kline, 2005] Kline, R. (2005). *Principles and Practice of Structural Equation Modeling*. The Guilford Press, second edition.

[Kosslyn, 1989] Kosslyn, S. (1989). Understanding charts and graphs. *Applied Cognitive Psychology*, 3(3):185–225.

[Kosslyn, 1985] Kosslyn, S. M. (1985). Graphics and human information processing. *Journal of the American Statistical Association*, 80(391):185–226.

[Kosslyn, 2002] Kosslyn, S. M. (2002). Display design for the eye and mind. In *Proceedings of the IEEE Symposium on Information Visualization (InfoVis'02)*, INFOVIS '02, pages 171–179, Washington, DC, USA. IEEE Computer Society.

[Krogstie, 2003] Krogstie, J. (2003). Evaluating uml using a generic quality framework. In *UML and the unified process*, pages 1–22. IGI Publishing.

[Kuutti, 1995] Kuutti, K. (1995). Activity theory as a potential framework for human-computer interaction research.

[Lansdale, 1988] Lansdale, M. (1988). On the memorability of icons in an information retrieval task. *Behaviour and Information Technology*, 7(2):131–151.

[Larkin and Simon, 1987] Larkin, J. and Simon, H. (1987). Why a diagram is (sometimes) worth ten thousand words. *Cognitive Science*, 11(1):65–100.

[Leontiev, 1978] Leontiev, A. N. (1978). *Activity, consciousness and personality*. Prentice Hall, Englewood Cliffs, NJ.

[Lindgaard, 2007] Lindgaard, G. (2007). Aesthetics, visual appeal, usability and user satisfaction: What do the user's eyes tell the user's brain? *Australian Journal of Emerging Technologies and Society*, 5(1):1–14.

[Lohmöller, 1989] Lohmöller, L. (1989). *Latent Variable Path Modeling with Partial Least Squares*. Springer, Berlin , New York.

[Lohse, 1993] Lohse, G. L. (1993). A cognitive model for understanding graphical perception. *Human Computer Interaction*, 8(4):353–388.

[Lohse, 1997] Lohse, G. L. (1997). The role of working memory in graphical information processing. *Behaviour and Information Technology*, 16(6):297–308.

[Loy, 1990] Loy, P. (1990). A comparison of object-oriented and structured development methods. *SIGSOFT Softw. Eng. Notes*, 15(1):44–48.

[Ludewig, 2003] Ludewig, J. (2003). Models in software engineering - an introduction. *Software and Systems Modeling*, 2(1):5–14.

[Lynn, 2006] Lynn, R. (2006). Solutions for missing data in structural equation modeling. *Research and Practice in Assessment*, 1(1):52–58.

[Mackinlay, 1986] Mackinlay, J. (1986). Automating the design of graphical presentations of relational information. *ACM Transactions On Graphics*, 5(2):110–141.

[Maes and Poels, 2007] Maes, A. and Poels, G. (2007). Evaluating quality of conceptual modelling scripts based on user perceptions. *Data and Knowledge Engineering*, 63(1):701–724.

[Mayer and Moreno, 2003] Mayer, R. and Moreno, R. (2003). Nine ways to reduce cognitive load in multimedia learning. *Educational Psychologist*, 38(1):43–52.

[Mayer, 1989] Mayer, R. E. (1989). Models for understanding. *Review of Educational Research*, 59(1):43–64.

[Mc Cabe, 1976] Mc Cabe, T. J. (1976). A complexity measure. *IEEE Transactions on Software Engineering*, 2(4):308–320.

[Mendling, 2008] Mendling, J. (2008). *Metrics for process models: Empirical foundations of verification, error prediction, and guidelines for correctness*, volume 6. Springer, Berlin, Heidelberg, New York, NY.

[Mendling and Strembeck, 2008] Mendling, J. and Strembeck, M. (2008). Influence factors of understanding business process models. *Proceedings of the 11th International Conference on Business Information Systems*, 7(1):142–153.

[Mitchell and Jolley, 2001] Mitchell, M. and Jolley, J. (2001). *Research Design Explained*, volume 4. Harcourt, New York.

[Moody, 2009] Moody, D. (2009). The "physics" of notations: Toward a scientific basis for constructing visual notations in software engineering. *IEEE Transactions on Software Engineering*, 35(6):756–779.

[Moody, 2004] Moody, D. L. (2004). Theoretical and practical issues in evaluating the quality of conceptual models: current state and future directions. *Data and Knowledge Engineering*, 55:243–276.

[Moody and Heymans, 2010] Moody, D. L. and Heymans, P. (2010). Visual syntax does matter: improving the cognitive effectiveness of the i* visual notation. *Requirements Engineering*, 15(1):141–175.

[Moody and Hillegersberg, 2009] Moody, D. L. and Hillegersberg, J. (2009). Evaluating the visual syntax of uml: An analysis of the cognitive effectiveness of the uml family of diagrams. *Lecture Notes in Computer Science*, 5452(1):16–34.

[Mylopoulos et al., 1978] Mylopoulos, J., Bernstein, P. A., and Wong, H. K. T. (1978). A language facility for designing interactive database-intensive applications. In *Proceedings of the 1978 ACM SIGMOD International Conference on Management of Data*, pages 17–17. ACM.

[Nembhard and Napassavong, 2002] Nembhard, D. and Napassavong, O. (2002). Task complexity effects on between-individual learning/forgetting variability. *International Journal of Industrial Ergonomics*, 29(2):297–306.

[Nembhard and Uzumeri, 2000] Nembhard, D. and Uzumeri, M. (2000). Experimental learning and forgetting for manual and cognitive tasks. *International Journal of Industrial Ergonomics*, 25(2):315–326.

[Nielsen, 1993] Nielsen, J. (1993). *Usability Engineering*. Morgan Kaufmann, 1st edition.

[Nielsen, 2006a] Nielsen, J. (2006a). *Prioritizing Web usability*. New Riders.

[Nielsen, 2006b] Nielsen, J. (2006b). Quantitative studies: How many users to test?

[Nunnally and Bernstein, 1994] Nunnally, J. and Bernstein, I. (1994). *Psychometric Theory*. McGraw-Hill Humanities/Social Sciences/Languages, 3 edition.

[Oei et al., 1992] Oei, J., van Hemmen, L., Falkenberg, L., and Brinkkemper, S. (1992). The meta model hierarchy: A framework for information systems concepts and techniques. *Technical Report No. 92-17*, pages 1–30.

[Olle et al., 1986] Olle, T., Sol, H., and Verijin-Stuart, A. (1986). A comparative evaluation of system development methods.

[OMG, 2005a] OMG (2005a). Introduction to omg's unified modeling language™ (uml®). Technical report, Object Management Group.

[OMG, 2005b] OMG (2005b). Unified modeling language. Technical report, Object Management Group.

[OMG, 2011a] OMG (2011a). Business process model and notation (bpmn 2.0). Technical report, Object Management Group, http://www.omg.org/spec/BPMN/2.0/PDF.

[OMG, 2011b] OMG (2011b). Meta object facility (mof) core specification. Technical report, Object Management Group, http://www.omg.org/spec/MOF/2.4.1/PDF.

[OMG, 2011c] OMG (2011c). Unified modeling language infrastructure. Version 2.4.1, Object Management Group, http://www.omg.org/spec/UML/2.4/Infrastructure/Beta2/PDF/.

[OMG, 2011d] OMG (2011d). Unified modeling language superstructure. Technical report, Object Management Group, http://www.omg.org/spec/UML/2.4.1/Superstructure/PDF/.

[Paivio, 1986] Paivio, A. (1986). *Mental representations: a dual coding approach.* Oxford University Press, Oxford.

[Palmer and Rock, 1994] Palmer, S. and Rock, I. (1994). Rethinking perceptual organization: The role of uniform connectedness. *Psychonomic Bulletin; Review,* 1:29–55. 10.3758/BF03200760.

[Pan et al., 2004] Pan, B., Hembrooke, H. A., Gay, G. K., Granka, L. A., Feusner, M. K., and Newman, J. K. (2004). The determinants of web page viewing behavior: an eye-tracking study. *Proceedings of the 2004 symposium on Eye tracking research and ypplication,* pages 147–154.

[Parnas, 1972] Parnas, D. (1972). A technique for software module specification with examples. *Communications of the ACM,* 15(5):330–336.

[Pearl, 2000] Pearl, J. (2000). *Causality: Models, Reasoning, and Inference.* Cambridge University Press.

[Petre, 2006] Petre, M. (2006). Cognitive dimensions 'beyond the notation'. *Journal of Visual Languages and Computing,* 17(4):292–301.

[Pfeiffer, 2007] Pfeiffer, D. (2007). Constructing comparable conceptual models with domain specific languages. In *Proceedings of the 15th European Conference on Information Systems (ECIS2007),* St.Gallen, Switzerland.

[Plass et al., 2010] Plass, J., Moreno, R., and Brünken, R. (2010). *Cognititve Load Theory.* Cambridge University Press.

[Pohl, 1994] Pohl, K. (1994). The three dimensions of requirements engineering. In *CAISE93 Selected papers from the fifth international conference on Advanced information systems engineering*, pages 275–292. Springer.

[Preece et al., 1994] Preece, J., Rogers, Y., Sharp, H., Benyon, D., Holland, S., and Carey, T. (1994). *Human Computer Interaction*. Addison-Wesley, Wokingham.

[Pretorius et al., 2005] Pretorius, M. C., Calitz, A. P., and van Greunen, D. (2005). The added value of eye tracking in the usability evaluation of a network management tool. In *Proceedings of the annual Research Conference of the South African Institute for Computer Scientists and Information Technologists*, pages 1–10. South African Institute for Computer Scientists and Information Technologists.

[Recker and Dreiling, 2007] Recker, J. C. and Dreiling, A. (2007). Does it matter which process modelling language we teach or use? an experimental study on understanding process modelling languages without formal education. In *Proceedings of 18th Australasian Conference on Information System (ACIS 2007)*. University of Southern Queensland.

[Recker et al., 2006] Recker, J. C., Indulska, M., Rosemann, M., and Green, P. (2006). How good is bpmn really? insights from theory and practice. In Ljungberg, J. and Andersson, M., editors, *14th European Conference on Information Systems (ECIS)*, pages 178–190.

[Recker et al., 2009] Recker, J. C., Zur Muehlen, M., Keng, S., Erickson, J., and Indulska, M. (2009). Measuring method complexity: Uml versus bpmn. *Proceedings of the Fifteenth Americas Conference on Information Systems, San Francisco, California*.

[Reijers and Vanderfeesten, 2005] Reijers, H. and Vanderfeesten, I. (2005). Cohesion and coupling metrics for workflow process design. *Lecture Notes in Computer Science*, 3080(1):290–305.

[Rengger et al., 1993] Rengger, R., Macleod, M., Bowden, R., Blaney, M., and Bevan, N. (1993). *MUSiC Performance Measurement Handbook*. National Physical Laboratory, Teddington, UK.

[Ringle et al., 2011] Ringle, C. M., Wende, S., and Will, A. (2011). Smartpls.

[Ross, 1977] Ross, D. (1977). Structured analysis: A language for communicating ideas. *IEEE Transactions on Software Engineering*, 3(1):16–34.

[Rossi and Brinkkemper, 1996] Rossi, M. and Brinkkemper, S. (1996). Complexity metrics for systems development methods and techniques. *Information Systems*, 21(2):209–227.

[Roussopoulos and Yeh, 1984] Roussopoulos, N. and Yeh, H. (1984). An adaptable methodology for database design. *ACM Transactions on Database Systems*, 17(5):64–80.

[Schafer and Graham, 2002] Schafer, J. and Graham, J. (2002). Missing data: Our view of the state of the art. *Psychological Methods*, 7(2):147–177.

[Schalles et al., 2010a] Schalles, C., Creagh, J., and Rebstock, M. (2010a). Developing a usability evaluation framework (fueml) for modeling languages. In Fox, R. and Golubski, W., editors, *Proceedings of the IASTED International Conference on Software Engineering (SE)*, volume 3, pages 126–135, Innsbruck. Acta Press.

[Schalles et al., 2010b] Schalles, C., Creagh, J., and Rebstock, M. (2010b). Ein generischer ansatz zur messung der benutzerfreundlichkeit von modellierungssprachen. In Engels, G., Karagiannis, D., and Mayr, H. C., editors, *Modellierung 2010*, volume 161 of *Lecture Notes in Informatics (LNI)*, pages 15–30, Klagenfurt. Gesellschaft für Informatik (GI).

[Schalles et al., 2010c] Schalles, C., Creagh, J., and Rebstock, M. (2010c). A generic metric for measuring complexity of models. In Filipe, J. and Cordeiro, J., editors, *Proceedings of the 12th International Conference on Enterprise Information Systems (ICEIS)*, volume 3, pages 436–439, Funchal (Madeira).

[Schalles et al., 2011a] Schalles, C., Creagh, J., and Rebstock, M. (2011a). Experiences on using partial least squares in usability research. In Bleimann, U., Walsh, P., and Humm, B., editors, *Proceedings of the 2nd Collaborative European Research Conference (CERC)*, volume 2, pages 7–18, Cork.

[Schalles et al., 2011b] Schalles, C., Creagh, J., and Rebstock, M. (2011b). Usability of modelling languages for model interpretation: An empirical research report. In Bernstein, A. and Schwabe, G., editors, *Proceedings of the 10th International Conference on Wirtschaftsinformatik (WI2011)*, volume 2, pages 787–797, Zurich.

[Schalles et al., 2012] Schalles, C., Creagh, J., and Rebstock, M. (2012). Exploring usability-driven differences of graphical modeling languages: An empirical research report. In Sinz, E., editor, *Lecture Notes in Informatics (LNI)*, volume 201, pages 91–106, Bamberg.

[Scheer, 1992] Scheer, A.-W. (1992). *Architecture of Integrated Information Systems: Principles of Enterprise Modeling*. Springer Berlin Heidelberg.

[Schuette and Rotthowe, 1998] Schuette, R. and Rotthowe, T. (1998). *The Guidelines of Modeling - An Approach to Enhance the Quality in Information Models*, volume 1507 of *Lecture Notes in Computer Science (LNCS)*, pages 240–254. Springer.

[Schwanenflugel and Shoben, 1983] Schwanenflugel, P. and Shoben, E. (1983). Differential context effects in the comprehension of abstract and concrete verbal materials. *Journal of Experimental Psychology*, 9(1):82–102.

[Seffah et al., 2006] Seffah, A., Donyaee, M., Kline, R., and Padda, H. (2006). Usability measurement and metrics: A consolidated model. *Software Quality Control*, 14(2):159–178.

[Shackel, 1991] Shackel, B. (1991). Usability - context, framework, definition, design and evaluation. In Shackel, B. and Richardson, S., editors, *Human Factors for Informatics Usability*, pages 21–38. University Press, Cambridge.

[Shaft and Vessey, 2006] Shaft, T. and Vessey, I. (2006). The role of cognitive fit in the relationship between software comprehension and modification. *MIS Quarterly*, 30(1):29–55.

[Shannon et al., 1998] Shannon, C., Weaver, W., and Shannon (1998). *The Mathematical Theory of Communication*. University of Illinois Press.

[Siau and Cao, 2001] Siau, K. and Cao, Q. (2001). Unified modeling language (uml) - a complexity analysis. *Journal of Database Management*, 12(1):26–34.

[Siau and Loo, 2006] Siau, K. and Loo, P.-P. (2006). Identifying difficulties in learning uml. *IS Management*, 23(3):43–51.

[Siau and Rossi, 2008] Siau, K. and Rossi, M. (2008). Evaluation techniques for systems analysis and design modelling methods; a review and comparative analysis. *Information Systems Journal*.

[Siau and Wang, 2007] Siau, K. and Wang, Y. (2007). Cognitive evaluation of information modeling methods. *Information and Software Technology*, 49(5):455–474.

[Sibert and Jacob, 2000] Sibert, L. E. and Jacob, R. J. (2000). Evaluation of eye gaze interaction. In *Proceedings of the SIGCHI conference on Human factors in computing systems*, pages 281–288. ACM.

[Sjoberg et al., 2007] Sjoberg, D., Dyba, T., and Jorgensen, M. (2007). The future of empirical methods in software engineering research. *Future of Software Engineering*, pages 358–378.

[Smith and Smith, 1977] Smith, J. M. and Smith, D. C. P. (1977). Database abstractions: aggregation and generalization. *ACM Transactions on Database Systems*, 2:105–133.

[Sonderegger and Sauer, 2009] Sonderegger, A. and Sauer, J. (2009). The influence of design aesthetics in usability testing: Effects on user performance and perceived usability. *Applied Ergonomics*, 41(3):403–410.

[Stachowiak, 1973] Stachowiak, H. (1973). *Allgemeine Modelltheorie*. Springer, Wien.

[Stevens, 1999] Stevens, J. (1999). *Intermediate Statistics - A Modern Approach*. Lawrence Erlbaum, page 77, London.

[Stevens, 2001] Stevens, J. (2001). *Applied Multivariate Statistics for the Social Sciences (Applied Multivariate STATS)*. Lawrence Erlbaum.

[Strom, 1986] Strom, R. (1986). A comparison of the object-oriented and process paradigms.

[Sweller, 2005] Sweller, J. (2005). Implications of cognititve load theory for multimedia learning. In Mayer, R. E., editor, *The Cambridge Handbook of Multimedia Learning*. Cambridge University Press, Cambridge.

[Tamir et al., 2008] Tamir, D., Komogortsev, O. V., and Mueller, C. J. (2008). An effort and time based measure of usability. In *Proceedings of the 6th international Workshop on Software Quality (WoSQ'08)*. ACM. 1370111 47-52.

[Tenenhaus et al., 2005] Tenenhaus, M., Vinzi, V., Chatelin, Y., and Lauro, C. (2005). Pls path modeling. *Computational statistics and Data analysis*, 48(2):159–205.

[Treisman, 1982] Treisman, A. (1982). Perceptual grouping and attention in visual search for features and for objects. *Journal of Experimental Psychology*, 8:194–214.

[Underwood, 2005] Underwood, G. D. (2005). *Cognititve Processes in Eye Guidance*. Oxford University Press, New York.

[Underwood, 2009] Underwood, G. D. (2009). Cognitive processes in eye guidance: Algorithms for attention in image processing. *Cognititve Computation*, 1(1):64–76.

[Vanderfeesten et al., 2007a] Vanderfeesten, I., Cardoso, J., Mendling, J., Reijers, H., and Van der Aalst, W. (2007a). Quality metrics for business process models. In Fischer, L., editor, *Workflow Handbook 2007*. Workflow Management Coalition, Lighthouse Point, Florida.

[Vanderfeesten et al., 2007b] Vanderfeesten, I., Cardoso, J., and Reijers, H. (2007b). A weighted coupling metric for business process models. In *The 19th International Conference on Advanced Information Systems Engineering (CAiSE'07)*, Trondheim, Norway.

[Vogt, 1999] Vogt, W. P. (1999). *Dictionary of Statistics and Methodology - A nontechnical guide for the social Sciences*. Sage Publications, California.

[Vuolle et al., 2008] Vuolle, M., Aula, A., Kulju, M., and Vainio, T. (2008). Identifying usability and productivity dimensions for measuring the success of mobile business services. *Advances in Human-Computer Interaction*.

[Wahl and Sindre, 2005] Wahl, T. and Sindre, G. (2005). An analytical evaluation of bpmn using a semiotic quality framework.

[Walker et al., 1998] Walker, M., Fromer, J., Di Fabbrizio, G., Mestel, C., and Hindle, D. (1998). What can i say?: evaluating a spoken language interface to email. pages 582–589.

[Wallenburg and Weber, 2005] Wallenburg, C. M. and Weber, J. (2005). Structural equation modeling as a basis for theory development within logistics and supply chain management research. In Kotzab, H., Seuring, S., Müller, M., and Reiner, G., editors, *Research Methodologies in Supply Chain Management*. Springer Berlin Heidelberg.

[Wand and Weber, 1993] Wand, Y. and Weber, R. (1993). On the ontological expressiveness of information systems analysis and design grammars. *Information Systems Journal*, 3(4):217–237.

[Weiber and Mühlhaus, 2009] Weiber, R. and Mühlhaus, D. (2009). *Strukturgleichungsmodellierung*. Springer, Heidelberg.

[Welke, 1992] Welke, R. (1992). The case repository: more than another database application. In Cottermann, W. and Senn, J., editors, *Challenges and strategies for research in systems development*, pages 181–218. Wiley Inc.

[Wertheimer, 1938] Wertheimer, M. (1938). *Laws of organization in perceptual forms*, pages 71–88. Routledge and Kegan Paul.

[Werts et al., 1974] Werts, C. E., Linn, R. L., and Jöreskog, K. G. (1974). Intraclass reliability estimates: Testing structural assumptions. *Educational and Psychological Measurement*, 34(1):25–33.

[Westphal and Würtz, 2009] Westphal, G. and Würtz, R. (2009). Combining feature-and correspondence-based methods for visual object recognition. *Neural Computation*, 21(7):1952–1989.

[Weyuker, 1988] Weyuker, E. (1988). Evaluating software complexity measures. *Software Engineering, IEEE Transactions on*, 14(9):1357–1365.

[Winn, 1990] Winn, W. (1990). Encoding and retrieval of information in maps and diagrams. *Professional Communication, IEEE Transactions on*, 33(3):103–107.

[Winn, 2002] Winn, W. (2002). An account of how readers search for information in diagrams. *Contemporary Educational Psychology*, 18(2):162–185.

[Withrow, 1990] Withrow, C. (1990). Error density and size in ada software. *Software, IEEE*, 7(1):26–30.

[Wold, 1980] Wold, H. (1980). Model construction and evaluation when theoretical knowledge is scare: theory and application of partial least squares. In Kmenta, J. and Ramsey, J., editors, *Evaluation of econometric models*. Academic Press, New York.

[Yang et al., 2006] Yang, Z., Zhang, D., and YE, C. (2006). Evaluation metrics for ontology complexity and evolution analysis. In *Proceedings of the IEEE International Conference on e-Business Engineering*, pages 162–170. IEEE Computer Society.

[Yau and Collofello, 1985] Yau, S. S. and Collofello, J. S. (1985). Design stability measures for software maintenance. *IEEE Transactions on Software Engineering*, 11(9):849–856.

Nomenclature

AVE	Average Variance Extracted
BPMN	Business Process Modeling Notation
EPC	Event Driven Process Chains
FUEML	Framework for Usability Evaluation of Modeling Languages
GCMM	Generic Metric for Measuring Model Complexity
SADT	Structured Analysis and Design Technique
SEM	Structural Equation Model
UML	Unified Modeling Language
XPDL	XML Process Definition Language

Glossary

Analysis of Covariance

Analysis of covariance is a statistical method that allows to compare one variable in two or more groups.

Behavioral Model

Illustrates the behavior of a system.

Graphical Model

A graphical representation i.e. diagram of a software system or a business process.

Partial Least Squares

A statistical method for calculating sturctural equation models.

(Business) Process Model

A graphical representation of a business process or a software process.

Structural Model

Defines the structural relations between latent variables within a sturctural equation model.

Structural Equation Modeling

A statistical technique for testing and estimating causal relations using a combination of statistical data and qualitative causal assumptions.